Life in Old Sodus

by
Michael Leonard Jewell

To the Lord Jesus Christ—my Savior, Comforter, Creator, Hero, and Friend.

To my uncles—
Sheriff Forrest L. Jewell and
Chief Deputy Donald E. Jewell of the Berrien County Sheriff's Department, retired.

To the men of the United States Army Special Forces who have captured my imagination—
in particular, Captain Nicholas J. Hun and First Sergeant Bobby W. "Claymore" Brown, my CO and First Sergeant, 411th Military Police Company, 720th Military Police Battalion, Fort Hood, Texas, and those other Green Berets I had the privilege to work with at Fort Chaffee, Arkansas, who served as Vietnamese interpreters.

Table of Contents

River School · 1
Joe · 12
The Elusive Studebaker ·. 22
King's Landing · 25
Joe and the Farm · 43
Brenda's Challenge · 49
Lien Shows Them She Understands · 56
Thoughts Turn to Other Things · 67
The Fireman's Picnic · 72
A Worthwhile Investment · 82
The Final Straw · 88
Making Joe Understand · 92
A Fine Lady · 105
Brenda Gets a Visit · 114
Facing Their Worst Fears · 125
Mrs. Holloway Has a Secret · 130
The Mission · 142
The Hunter · 149
Reversing the Fear · 162
Mending Fences · 169
Andy and Sarah's Mystery · 178
Mrs. Holloway Has a Surprise · 196
Pleasant It Was · 207

One
River School

East of Sodus near the tiny hamlet of Shanghai stood an old, decaying farmhouse, lonely and drear. Set far off a brown gravel road, its vast yard was choked with weeds and tall grass that had long gone to seed. Scattered here and there among the blackberry brambles were piles of firewood cut from old fruit trees. Next to the barn in uneven rows piled worn-out farm machinery, long forsaken and left to rust. A large galvanized mailbox stood by the road, mounted upon a crooked grape post, dented and marred with buckshot holes. A rusted 1938 Chevrolet, up on concrete blocks and without a windshield, was parked at the edge of the vegetable garden. Except for the telltale smoke and sparks of a blazing wood fire spewing forth from its red brick chimney, the house appeared to be abandoned.

Inside the house, seated next to the kitchen window in a white, tall-backed chair, was an old man with a careworn face and grizzled beard. His gray hair was shaggy and his faded bib overalls soiled and stained from many years of labor on his modest estate. He sat motionless, staring into the shadowy room, gripping a tin cup of black coffee that had grown cold. The sun had long set, and a smoky lantern, once painted bright red, sat solitary on an old wooden kitchen table.

Loosening his grip on his cup, the old man leaned forward and peered through the glass of the curtainless window, but he saw nothing in the blackness of the moonless night. He paused again and cocked his head as a bird would do, listening intently for the sound of a key at the lock or a footstep at the back door.

"Georgie, won't ya come ta bed? It ain't good for you ta sit up so late," said a woman's soft voice from the dark. "He'll be home soon. Please don't fret so."

"Jest a while longer, Maudie . . . a while longer," he replied as an ancient wooden mantel clock struck off eleven chimes.

The old man stirred from his seat and began pacing the bare wooden floor. Then, in a fit of anguish, he snatched his hat and ragged denim coat from a nail on the wall. Quickly grasping the wire handle of the lantern, he opened the door and dashed out into the wild, windy night. Stopping at the edge of the gravel road, he strained his eyes both ways in the darkness.

Nothing.

Life in Old Sodus

He sighed and began to walk up and down the road. His crunching footsteps on the wet stones and coarse brown earth were silent against the subtle moan of the bitter wind in the trees. At last, succumbing to the cold, he walked back into the house and resumed his lonely vigil in front of the window, warming his hands over the lantern.

* * *

The chilly Michigan air settled like a veil upon the orchards and vineyards of Sodus Township, leaving the tender buds to shiver upon their branches. The blustery March wind had abated, and a light frost had formed in low places. A flock of cedar waxwings buzzed and shrilled in the giant cottonwood tree near the railroad tracks in the center of town as the village slowly came to life.

Amberley and Brenda Bridges tried not to let the back door slam as they left the toasty warmth of the kitchen to unlock their bikes from the metal rail along the cement steps.

"Here, girls," Ma said, opening the door and handing them a towel. "Wipe the moisture off the seats so you don't get wet and catch your deaths."

"Thanks, Ma," they said and quickly mounted their bikes for the long ride to River School just beyond King's Landing.

Mary Bridges stepped out onto the back steps to retrieve the wet towel and watch as her daughters peddled out of sight. It had been over two years since she and Sam had adopted Brenda, whose mother had been a Pottawatomi Indian and whose father was a scoundrel ordered to leave Michigan by the courts for abuse and neglect. Their family had again increased when they adopted the little Vietnamese orphan, Lien. Amberley, their only natural daughter, with her red hair and freckles, often remarked with a smile that the Bridges family was in the habit of taking in "stray cats." But the girls riding away now looked beautiful and well cared for. *Not strays at all*, Mary thought to herself. *It's as if they have all always been my girls!*

As the bright sun steadily warmed the air, newly arrived red-winged blackbirds, with their bright epaulets of red and yellow, called out to their ladies among the cattails in the marshy ditches along Naomi Road. A great blue heron with its motionless silhouette, infinite in patience on its stilted legs, took a stab at a leopard frog.

The cool air was uncomfortable on the girls' faces as they peddled hard, making their eyes flow and their noses run. They were both loath to speak until Amberley finally broke the silence.

"We are nearly at the end of our sophomore year, and I'm getting tired of riding bikes to school like little girls. We'll be a couple of wrecks by the time we get there!" she said as they drove through a slushy mud puddle. "Do you know how far it is from home to school?"

"Not exactly, but I've heard that it's almost two miles one way. We're old enough to get our driver's licenses. Do you think the folks will let us take the truck to school sometime?"

"I don't know. Dad needs it for work. Maybe soon we can get a car of our own and share it, but that takes money, and we haven't any. It looks like we are going to be on our bikes until we graduate."

As the girls approached the school on River Road, Amberley remembered that a new teacher was starting that day at River School. Mr. Johnson had decided to retire early. He would be helping his son run his hardware store in Sister Lakes.

"I guess nothing ever stays the same, Brenda. What good does it do to get attached to something or someone when you know that it will just eventually go away?" Amberley said.

"Are you speaking of Mr. Johnson? He just wants to spend time with his son while he is still able."

Amberley sighed as she ran her fingers through her wind-tangled hair. "Oh, it's just everything. Our teachers, our friends—you and I will someday part. I guess I thought we would be together always. Now I'm growing up, and I know it ain't so."

Brenda slid her front wheel into the bike rack in front of the school. "We may part down here, someday, but not forever. We will always be sisters, and nothing can ever change that." Brenda bent down to tie a loose shoestring. "Besides, if everyone thought like that, no one would ever get married."

"Well, you're the only one with a prospect," Amberley teased.

"If you're referring to Joe Schenkle, we are just friends. There are a lot of nice boys around. Try being nicer, and perhaps one of them will talk to you," Brenda retorted.

"I don't know what you're talking about!" Amberley laughed. "I'm always nice!"

The girls entered the dark red brick building of River School, and each went to her separate classroom. Amberley went to her homeroom and found her old seat in front of the window. She was early—not even the new teacher was in yet. Amberley read her name on the blackboard: *Mrs. Davison.*

Another new teacher, she thought, and shook her head.

Amberley was staring out of the window, contemplating the beginning of class, when she heard a familiar voice behind her.

"Attention! Attention, please! Class is now in session!"

Amberley whirled about in her seat, and there, laughing almost uncontrollably, was Miss Collins.

"Miss Collins!" Amberley said. "You're back!"

She jumped to her feet and hugged the pretty teacher good and hard. Miss Collins was still laughing.

"Yes, dear! I moved away to go back to college and get my master's degree, but I couldn't stay away from Sodus. I thought I would try teaching high school. Will you welcome me back?"

"Of course, Miss Collins!"

"But I'm not Miss Collins anymore."

Amberley shook her head in happy confusion.

"Do you remember Mr. Davison who used to attend church in Sodus?"

"Yes, ma'am," she said, still not making the connection.

"Well, Mr. Davison and I were married last summer. I am now Margaret Davison. You didn't know because I kept it a secret and lived for today so I could tease you."

Amberley couldn't contain her happiness, and she hugged Teacher again. She whispered, "I've missed you so much, and I have never forgotten you."

Mrs. Davison swallowed hard. "I know—I've missed you too."

* * *

The girls rode their bikes home from school that afternoon. Amberley was in such a hurry to see Ma and tell her about Mrs. Davison that she forgot to explain the new teacher to Brenda. She let her bike drop to the ground by the mailbox, and running up the steps, she burst into the kitchen. Her mother had her back to the door and was setting the table.

"Ma! Ma! Guess who our new teacher is?" Amberley shouted, almost out of breath.

Ma wheeled around with a smile on her face. "Is it a mean old lady with thick-rimmed glasses?"

"No, Ma. It's Miss Collins, but her name isn't Miss Collins anymore. It's Mrs. Davison and . . ." Amberley's voice tapered off as she stood with her mouth open. "Oh, Ma! You knew, didn't you?"

Ma leaned forward and gave her daughter a peck on the forehead. "Yes, I knew. I kept it to myself because I wanted it to be a wonderful surprise for you."

Brenda was silent but listened intently. She had not known Mrs. Davison as Miss Collins.

"Amber, maybe you should tell Brenda all about Miss Collins while I finish getting dinner on the table," Ma said as she drained a pot of boiled potatoes into the sink.

The girls took their books upstairs to their bedroom and changed clothes for supper. Amberley told Brenda the story of her old run-ins with a far meaner, more insecure Miss Collins—until Amberley's witness and Ma's friendship had led Margaret Collins back to the Lord and changed her life.

"You see, Brenda, the Miss Collins I first met at Sodus School was not the sweet person you see now. God changed her life—little by little. And now she will be my teacher again, perhaps yours too, for the remainder of the school year."

Brenda listened and laughed at the funnier parts of the tale. "That's such a good story, Amber. She seems like a nice lady. I look forward to her being my teacher too!" She smiled and smoothed out her bed. She had not really made it known, but she had a secret desire to teach. It seemed that Mrs. Davison had been through a lot in her journey as a teacher and might be willing to share her wisdom. *Perhaps when I know her better,* Brenda thought.

"Supper's on," Ma called up the stairs. "Your father is home."

Sam walked in the back door and set his black lunch box on the counter. Close behind him, carrying his thermos bottle, was their adopted Vietnamese daughter, Lien. Sam had picked her up from Sodus School on his way home from work in Eau Claire.

"Hello, my sisters!" Lien said with an ear-to-ear grin, waving to them with an open hand. Her sweet little round face was lost in the fur-lined hood of her winter coat.

"Hello, sweetie!" Amberley exclaimed, holding her arms open to give Lien a hug.

"Ooh, it's so good to see you!" Brenda said, hugging her too.

Lien still spoke occasionally in pidgin English, but her sentences were mostly complete, and she had only a slight accent. Lien was almost ten, but still so small. It was always a temptation to treat her as younger than she really was.

Sam washed his hands at the kitchen sink and dried them on the towel draped over the counter. He smiled at Amberley and Brenda, who each kissed him on the cheek as he pulled out his chair to sit down.

"Girls?" Ma scolded mildly. "Help Lien with her coat and sit down for dinner. The mashed potatoes are getting cold."

* * *

The rooster crowed loudly several times and began to pace back and forth on the frosty roof of the chicken house. Maudie Schenkle opened her eyes and stared at the bluish glow coming through the bedroom window. She had not slept well that night and was exhausted, but duty and habit prevailed, and she sat up on the edge of the bed. It was time to put on the coffee and make breakfast. She instinctively brushed her hand across the blanket on her husband's side of the bed. He was not there.

Maudie put on her faded terrycloth robe, and stepping into her slippers, made her way through the dim light of the growing dawn to the kitchen. As she walked through the narrow doorway, Maudie abruptly stopped. There, seated at the kitchen table before an empty kerosene lantern, was the old man she had married, sound asleep in his exhaustion. He was breathing heavily and resting his head against his folded arms on the table.

Maudie felt a tear run down her cheek as she hurried to his side and held him close.

"Oh, Georgie, what am I going to do with you?"

Two
Joe

It was a dismal Friday at school, for it had rained all day, and as the black clock with the white face struck three, the girls were anxious to get home. They closed their books and hurried to the exit door facing the St. Joseph River. Pounding rain and melting snow had made it swell its banks, and they could hear the rushing sound as it flowed swiftly northwest to Lake Michigan. They waited as long as they could in hopes that the rain would abate, but it continued to come down in steady sheets. Finally they acquiesced, and Amberley and Brenda pulled their hoods up over their heads and began the soggy journey home from River School. As they alternated peddling with walking to keep from falling on the slick roadway, they noticed that water was standing in the fields and along Naomi Road in large puddles.

The sisters were almost home when they spied a large black sedan driving swiftly toward them from the direction of town. They recognized it as belonging to Mrs. Holloway, the elderly widow from King's Landing. The girls had never met her face-to-face and knew little about her except that she was very rich and very mysterious. Dad had occasionally done odd jobs and carpentry work on her estate, but he rarely spoke of her.

The large black Bentley rumbled toward them, and Amberley wasn't sure if the driver was able to see them in the pouring rain. As the heavy car swished closely past them, the girls steered their bikes into the rain-swollen ditch to give it room. The car splashed a huge puddle, sending a rooster tail of muddy water high into the air. The girls were soaking wet, and as they crawled out of the ditch and retrieved their bikes, they could see the blurry taillights of Mrs. Holloway's car as it continued driving westward down the road, oblivious to what had been done.

** ***

Several weeks passed, and on one warm April Saturday morning, the Bridges family sat about their breakfast table. The sun was bright and illuminated the yellow walls of the kitchen. Mary's golden-brown buttermilk biscuits and sausage gravy were the morning fare, and the girls chatted among themselves about their plans for the day. Mary was to help Mrs. Enkins, the neighbor lady and wife of Sam's boss, with some baking for the church fellowship that Sunday afternoon.

Sam had planned on doing some repairs around the house and had just returned from the hardware store in Eau Claire. He sat down to breakfast and said nothing as he ate.

"Sam, you are certainly quiet this morning," Mary said with a smile.

Sam looked up. Everyone was staring at him. "I guess I am, Mary." He smiled back.

After pausing and taking a few more bites of food, he spoke. "Girls, have you seen Joe Schenkle lately? Does he still come to school?" he asked. He wasn't smiling now.

Amberley and Brenda looked at him, puzzled.

"Why no, Dad," Amberley said. "He hasn't been in school since before spring break."

Joe Schenkle was the farmer boy from Shanghai who had saved Mary's life several years ago during a raging blizzard. The Schenkles of Shanghai were legendary as troublemakers, and Joe himself had once reigned as the premier bully of Sodus School—taken down a peg only by Brenda, who wasn't above throwing a punch or two herself in those days.

"Sam, is there something wrong?" Mary asked soberly.

"When I was in town this morning," he said with a pause, "I heard that George Schenkle, Joe's father, passed away in the night. Rumor is that Joe hasn't been home for several days and isn't even aware that his dad is gone."

The room grew silent as everyone thought on the sad news. Finally, Mary spoke up. "Sam, please go find Joe. He is a good boy at heart, and I . . . we owe him so much."

"I'll look for him right after breakfast, but I'll go see his mother first," Sam said, picking at a biscuit crust with his fork.

"Give me time to make a meal for you to take along. I'm sure Maudie Schenkle isn't thinking about that. Poor Maudie . . . and Joe."

***

Sam drove out east of town in his pickup on Naomi Road to Shanghai. There were no comforters or well-wishers at the Schenkle farm when he arrived. He made his way through the cluttered yard with the basket of food Mary had prepared. As he knocked on the kitchen door, he noticed that his boots were muddy and wet with the dew.

"Good morning, Maudie," Sam said with a smile.

"Hello, Sam. Glad ta see ya. Won't you come on in?" she said, her eyes red with weeping.

Sam slipped his boots off at the door.

"I'm so sorry about George, Maudie. Has Pastor Mitchell been by yet?"

"Yes, Sam. He's just left. He'll be by later with Mrs. Mitchell to fetch me to Bowerman's to make arrangements."

Sam set the basket of food on the table as Maudie poured him a cup of black coffee.

"Thank you, Sam. Tell Mary thanks," she said.

Sam smiled and nodded his head as they sat for several moments in the silence of the rustic kitchen until the mantel clock struck off the hour. Suddenly, in a rush of emotion, Maudie blurted out her sorrow.

"Oh, Sam! What am I gonna do? George is gone, and Joe . . ."

Sam reached out and held Maudie's hand. She wept into her handkerchief as Sam remained silent, not knowing what to say.

"Where is Joe, Maudie?" he finally asked.

"I ain't seen him in days," she said, wiping her swollen eyes. "He comes and goes as it pleases him. He started missin' school a few weeks back and then staying out late. He's been runnin' around with that Michael McGuinnes what owns the sawmill. He's a bad lot, Sam. He seems to have put a spell on Joe and got him to believe he doesn't need ta finish school."

Sam frowned as if he had smelled something rotten. "I know McGuinnes, Maudie. Let me see if I can find Joe," he said as he stood from his chair. "I'll send him on home."

Sam drove south on the winding Park Road to the village of Eau Claire. He parked at the feed store by the railroad tracks and asked if anyone had seen Joe. Tim

Derby, the owner, was in the back room filling cloth sacks with chicken feed.

"I've seen 'im, Sam, off and on the last few days," he said, stitching a dusty sack closed and setting it against the wall. "He's been with Michael McGuinnes. If he was my boy, I'd box his ears for havin' anything to do with him."

"But what have they been doing?" Sam asked. "Where did you see him last?"

Derby paused and then squinted his eyes as if he was scrutinizing some distant mountain.

"Seems to me that I seen 'im comin' out of the tavern on the corner once or twice. Saw him this mornin', as a matter of fact."

"Thanks, Tim," Sam said as he walked out the door and stood staring at the Belmont Tavern on the corner. He knew it well: it was one of the haunts of his old days. He dreaded the thought of having to enter its doors once again. He cleared his throat and smoothed back his hair as he began the walk to the alley behind the tavern. Perhaps he could enter the back way and no one would see him. He hated to think of the rumors if the townsfolk saw him going inside—many still considered him nothing but an old drunk. Still, he had to see if Joe was there.

Sam stared at the heavy metal door of the alley entrance. It was rudely familiar, and flexing his fingers to overcome his apprehension, he yanked it open and walked in. The contrast with the bright sun made the room appear pitch black until his eyes adjusted to the light. He scanned the room, which was nearly empty except for a few people seated at the bar and scattered among the tables. Through the stale smell and haze of smoke, he could see two men sitting in the back corner. Sam approached their table and stood beside Joe, who was six foot three and at least two hundred and twenty pounds. He would be a handful if he decided not to come along.

"Joe, what are you doing in here?" Sam asked sternly.

Joe quickly looked up and then hung his head, embarrassed to make eye contact with Sam.

"He's with me, Bridges," Michael McGuinnes growled. "Now why don't you just leave him be?"

Sam ignored the man and continued. "Joe, I've been at your ma's. I told her I would bring you home."

Joe began to rise slowly from his chair.

"Hey! You don't have to go with him, Joe," McGuinnes said, standing up.

Sam reached out and pushed McGuinnes back into his chair. This surprised the scruffy sawmill owner, and he quickly stood up again with his fists at his side.

"Stay out of this, Mike," Sam warned.

"Or what?" McGuinnes sneered.

"Or it may be one of the biggest mistakes of your miserable life," Sam exclaimed, his blue eyes snapping.

McGuinnes was at first expressionless, but then he sat back in his chair with a saucy grin. He leaned back on two legs and placed a booted foot on the edge of the table.

"So, Sam Bridges, the big bad Green Beret! Haven't seen you in here for a long time. Have you come to have a drink? You must be mighty thirsty by now. Or did you come to preach us a sermon?"

The words smarted, but Sam said nothing as he turned to leave with Joe.

"What's the matter, Sam? No guts?" McGuinnes snarled.

Sam paused and then turned around. "It seems to me that I whipped you quite a few times when we were boys, and I didn't need a Green Beret to do it then. McGuinnes, you are what they call a classic ne'er-do-well. When faced with a clear decision to do right or wrong, you can always be counted on to choose the latter. You think you can buy or steal your own way whenever you want it. You have always been that way and probably always will be. You see Joe here? He's not for sale, and I want you to stay away from him. And if I find out that you gave him something to drink, I'll be back to see you." And with that, they exited the dingy room into the alley.

For a few minutes they said nothing, stalking out of the alley side by side. Joe breathed like he wanted to say something, but Sam spoke first, his voice soft. "Joe? I have to talk to you."

Joe bristled. "Mr. Bridges, I don't wanna go back home. I ain't steady thinkin' 'bout spendin' my life on the farm. McGuinnes was goin' to give me a job at his sawmill, and with good pay too! Besides, Pa doesn't love me or care about me. All I am to him is another hired hand!"

Sam put his hand on Joe's shoulder, pinning him against the brick wall of the tavern. "Joe, you haven't been home so you don't know. I have to tell you . . . your pa passed away last night in his sleep."

Joe's cocky expression quickly changed to that of a fool who has just spoken his mind without thinking. He stood there with his mouth partially open, and then suddenly, he burst into tears.

"Go ahead, Joe. There is no shame," Sam said tenderly, putting his arm around the boy and letting him weep. "Joe, I don't know what problems you had with your pa, but I know he loved you very much. He stayed up late many a night, waiting for you to come home. I saw him myself late into the evening, pacing in front of the house with his lantern, hoping to get a glimpse of you coming down the road. He loved you, boy, but perhaps he just didn't know how to show it."

"I . . . I didn't know," Joe said pitifully, gulping and making an effort to compose himself.

"Joe, I'm going to take you home to your ma. She needs you now, more than ever. There is no room now for fooling around. Whatever was wrong between you and your pa must be put behind. You have to step up to the plate now and be a man. Will you do it?"

"Yes sir," Joe said with a nod.

"And can I tell your teacher that you will be back in school as soon as possible?"

"Yes sir."

Sam squeezed his shoulder. "Then let's go home. Being a man starts today."

Three
The Elusive Studebaker

Sam came through the back door bringing the warm April wind in with him. He kissed Mary on the cheek and handed her a bag of groceries that he had just picked up at the store. He was obviously in a cheerful mood.

"Girls, I have some good news I think you might like to hear. Do you remember Mrs. Holloway, the widow living on River Road in King's Landing? Well, I saw her just a few minutes ago at the IGA. She's looking for someone to help her do odd jobs around her old house this spring. She specifically asked about you. Are you interested?"

The girls certainly did remember her, and their recent bath in a muddy rain-filled ditch was fresh in their minds. They exchanged a look, and Amberley sighed.

"Sure, Dad. If she needs some help, I don't mind," Amberley said, not looking up as she set the table.

"I'll help too, Dad," said Brenda, politely.

"Now this isn't for nothing, ladies," Sam said, noting their tone. "She's a widow, and I know you would help her just for the asking, but she insists on paying you something. I mentioned to her that perhaps this summer, I was going to start teaching you girls how to drive. She told me that if you would help her for a few Saturdays around the house, she would give you her husband's old Studebaker parked in the barn. I've seen it, and it needs some work, but I think it can be fixed up."

Amberley almost dropped the tray of biscuits she had pulled from the oven. Brenda turned quickly and knocked the pepper mill off the counter.

"Oh, Dad, can that be possible? Mrs. Holloway will give us a real car for helping her fix up her house?" Amberley cried out.

"That's right, but along with this car goes a lot of responsibility," Sam warned.

"Oh, Amber!" Brenda exclaimed. "Think what we could do with our own car. This would give us a way to find and keep a job so we can save for college. And I've always wanted to visit the big libraries in St. Joe and Benton Harbor. I could do so much studying there—get a head start on teacher's college—"

"Now, just hold on a second! This is going entirely too fast. Sam, isn't this a little sudden?" Mary asked.

"Let me finish, Mary! Now girls, I'm going to make sure I trust your driving before I let you behind the wheel by yourselves. Also, part of your responsibility will be to help in paying for gasoline, maintenance, and insurance.

Your mother and I can't afford to pay for all of that. You two are going to have to find a way to help pay your share of the expenses."

The girls looked at their father as their smiles fled away. They hadn't thought of the expenses of owning a car. Like little girls, they had taken for granted many of the things their parents provided for them. Apparently money did not grow on trees after all.

"That's the challenge, girls. Now let's eat. I'm starved," Sam said with a big grin.

Amberley and Brenda looked at each other, contemplating the elusive Studebaker that seemed to have just driven itself beyond their reach.

Four
King's Landing

Early Saturday morning was warm but overcast as Amberley and Brenda helped Ma with breakfast. She always tried to have a special breakfast on Saturday, and today was no exception. She made fried potatoes, golden-brown with green peppers and onions, and buttermilk biscuits and gravy made from Grandma Andrews's good pork sausage. There were scrambled eggs made in Ma's special way. She would lightly fry the eggs in butter, careful to only cook and stir the whites. Just before they were served, she would break the yokes and mix them in. This would make the flavor rich and delicate.

As breakfast was readied, the girls could think of nothing but Mrs. Holloway and King's Landing. This would be their first Saturday afternoon to help her around her house; they were perhaps one step closer to getting a real car.

"Amber, just think how nice it will be driving to school this winter," Brenda said. "I am so tired of tramping through the snow and ice."

"I thought Joe might give you a ride on his horse," Amberley chuckled.

"Well, if he does, guess who is going to be left walking?" Brenda shot back.

"Enough of that, girls," Ma said sternly. "Wait until you get your car first, and then you can tease about it."

It was then that they were taken completely by surprise when Dad made an announcement.

"Mary, I have decided to give the girls their first driving lesson this morning," he said, splitting a hot biscuit and ladling it with gravy.

The room grew silent except for the sound of frying potatoes. Amberley and Brenda looked at each other as they set the table, and their surprised faces turned into grins. Lien was seated at the kitchen table, sipping orange juice through a straw, and she looked up with a loud slurp. He didn't mean her too, did he?

"But Sam," Mary spoke, "this is so sudden. Are you sure the girls are ready?"

"Never mind, Mary. They will do just fine. They are a bit older than we were when we first learned to drive."

Over breakfast, the girls remembered that Dad's pickup truck had a manual transmission, and that made them nervous. They voiced their concerns to him about it, but he only smiled.

"There was a time, ladies, when all cars and trucks had standard transmissions. In my opinion, everybody ought to learn how to drive a stick before they drive an automatic. Anybody can just sit there and steer. It takes a real pro to work the clutch and gears."

"Sam!" Mary said with a serious smile. "You're scaring the girls by making it sound more complicated than it is. If I can learn to drive a standard transmission, so can they. I learned from driving Grandpa Andrews's old John Deere tractor, and I was years younger."

Ma put her hand over her mouth and started to chuckle. Her muffled, petite laugh always told them that she had remembered something funny from her past.

"What is it, Ma? Please tell us," Amberley asked.

"Oh, I was just remembering the first time I drove Grandpa's tractor. I was only about ten years old and always kind of a daredevil. My older brothers Fred and Junior were taunting me to get on the tractor and start the motor."

"Did you do it, Ma?" Amberley asked.

"I sure did. I probably would have climbed the corncrib and jumped off into the horse trough if they had dared me. Well, I scampered up onto the tractor seat wearing my sky-blue summer dress, pulled the choke like I'd seen your Grandpa do a hundred times, and pushed the starter button. It smoked and chugged away. I was so proud of myself, and I looked at my brothers with a smug face.

"Everything was going fine until Fred shouted out, 'Pa's comin' around the barn!' I went to jump off the tractor but forgot to shut it off. My dress caught on the gear stick and away the tractor went, out through Grandpa's freshly planted cornfield."

"Oh, Ma, what did you ever do?" Amberley said, setting down her fork.

"Fred and Junior ran alongside the tractor and tried to jump on to get it stopped. I was lying over the steering wheel, and every time I tried to sit up straight, the tractor would veer off to the left or right. At one point, the tractor was chasing them! I can remember crying so hard and looking back and seeing my mother standing on the porch wringing her hands. She was horrified, and I knew that if the tractor didn't kill me, I was going to get the lickin' of my life. The tank was full of gas, and I would probably still be out there if your grandpa hadn't jumped on Lucky, his old riding horse, and scooped me off in his arms. The tractor finally hit the corner of the barn and stopped dead."

"Oh, Ma! You were a regular juvenile delinquent," Brenda laughed as she refilled the coffee cups.

"I was to be sure," she chuckled. "Pa had to replant half an acre of corn and mend the corner of the barn. Fred and Junior weren't able to sit down for a week. Pa tanned their hides for daring me to do something so dangerous."

"Did Grandpa Andrews spank you, Ma?" Amberley asked.

"No, but Mom sure did! Pa handed me to her while he was still on Lucky. When she was sure I wasn't hurt, she took a switch from the willow tree at the corner of the yard and lit a fire under my boiler. After that, I tried to think about the consequences before I did anything so foolish and careless again. Now help me put away breakfast so your father can give you your first driving lesson."

When the chores were finished, Sam drove to the large field behind the post office and showed the girls how to steer and apply the brakes without bumping their heads against the windshield. The most difficult thing for the girls to master was operating the clutch without killing the engine. But Sam was a very patient teacher, and the girls were soon laughing and at ease.

Almost as quickly as it started, the first lesson was over. "Now you girls study those *Rules of the Road* booklets I gave you from the Secretary of State's office, and next week I will take you out and let you drive through an apple orchard. It will help you to get the feel of driving in town with corners and streets."

Amberley and Brenda helped Ma make a quick lunch of toasted cheese sandwiches and homemade tomato soup. While putting away the dishes, Ma declared that she was going to bake bread that afternoon while the girls were away.

"It would be nice, Sam, to have some good butter to go with the fresh hot bread."

"Wouldn't it though?" he answered. "I think I'll just drive over to the House of David Dairy and get a pound or two. I might as well get some buttermilk while I'm at it, if you will wash me out the glass jug."

The House of David Dairy on Territorial Road in Benton Harbor was one of the few places where anyone could still buy fresh, unpasteurized dairy products. The buttermilk and butter were sold ice-cold, and as far as they knew, everyone who purchased it remained healthy. Sam remarked that at one time, most of the old dairies were that way.

"I wish your ma still made her own butter and cheese," he said. "I know it got to be quite a handful for her as she got older and had to scale back production on the old farm."

"I miss it too," Mary said, handing him the glass gallon jug. "I'm glad that our kids at least get to taste a bit of the way it used to be."

Sam took Lien with him in the truck as Amberley and Brenda began the long bike ride to King's Landing. It was warm, and the yellow sun made the thin white cloud cover bright.

"What are we going to do, Brenda, about this car?" Amberley asked. "How can we afford to fix it up and pay for insurance and gasoline?"

"I don't know. I've been praying about it ever since Dad first told us. We're going to have to earn enough money somehow, but where are we going to get jobs? Even if Mrs. Holloway pays us something more, it won't cover the expenses."

"I thought about the IGA and the library, but people are already working both places. You know, Dad didn't seem too worried about it. Do you think he knows something we don't?" Amberley wondered.

"I think Dad just wants to see if we are resourceful. If the Lord wants us to have this car, He can certainly provide us a means to keep it. Anyway, we can always put it in the backyard and just sit in it," Brenda laughed.

Then Brenda grew serious. "Oh Amber, I'll just die if I can't go to college. We must do our best to earn this car. Then we can drive into town to get good jobs."

"I know, sis. If I think about it too much it upsets me, and Christians shouldn't be like that."

Mrs. Holloway's place was well off the road in the middle of a large tract of land overlooking the St. Joseph River. It was a grand old estate with a three-story Victorian house at its center. Its most striking feature was a tower that rose from the corner of the house and pierced into the sky. It could be seen for miles, and Dad had told them once that it housed an aviary, a place to keep birds many years ago when that sort of thing was stylish.

Brenda and Amberley had never met Mrs. Holloway except for the day she had splashed them several weeks ago. They saw her in town occasionally, where it was always odd to see her old black Bentley parked outside the plain brick IGA grocery store next to the fire station in Sodus.

Sam and his father had done work for the Holloways for many years. Grandpa Bridges had taught his son to be an expert carpenter, and they were among the few people allowed to enter the big house. Mrs. Holloway lived all alone except for her housekeeper and butler.

As the girls approached the estate, it seemed to loom over them and overshadow them. Surely someone with such a magnificent house had to be very rich and powerful. As the girls dismounted their bikes, Amberley leaned over to whisper to her sister.

"Brenda, when I was a little girl, I was told about two boys who went to trick-or-treat at Mrs. Holloway's and were never seen again."

Brenda paused and then looked at her sister with a frown. "Did you have to wait until now to tell me that, Amber? Is there anything else I need to know before it's too late?"

"I just thought you should know," Amberley chuckled.

As they walked their bikes up the long, tree-lined driveway, they couldn't help but realize how stately the place must have been in bygone years. The yard was vast and completely surrounded by a black wrought-iron fence. The grounds, with their many outbuildings and large stable, were shaded by ancient oaks and maples. There had once been a knot garden made of culinary herbs and a maze fashioned out of evergreen hedges and shrubbery. These were now a snarled forest of shapeless, unkempt vegetation, and the small fish pond and trickling fountain at its center was covered with duckweed and patches of chartreuse algae and scum.

At one corner of the yard was a spacious arbor covered by vines of grapes and hops. This must have provided cool shade for the many parties and cotillions that once were common on these grounds. It was not difficult to imagine the fine ladies in their long dresses sipping tea with their gentleman callers under the magnificent cascading greenery.

Amberley and Brenda were filled with vague apprehension as they walked up onto the porch that encircled the entire house. They suddenly felt so small, and the promise of an old dusty car unimportant. They could find no doorbell at the main entrance, and so, summoning her strength and taking a deep breath, Brenda knocked on the door. The wood was so heavy and solid that her small knuckles seemed to have no effect.

"I think we're supposed to rap the knocker," Amberley said.

Amberley reached up and tapped the heavy brass bar against the striker plate. It was shiny and beautiful, cast into the shape of a flying eagle carrying the bar in its feet. Amberley tapped it several more times, which sounded much too loud.

The girls stepped back from the door and waited in silence.

* * *

Sam and Lien soon returned from their errands in Benton Harbor. Mary was busy in the kitchen with her baking. Sam poured himself a cup of coffee and sat down at the kitchen table.

"Sam, do you think the girls will be all right? Mrs. Holloway is a little odd."

"Oh, I think so. I've been to her house dozens of times over the years with my pa and many times since." Then he chuckled under his breath. "She is a card, I will admit that. She acts as if she doesn't notice you, and when she does speak, it's in short sentences and commands. It's likely she's been accustomed to giving orders to servants all her life. I don't think she knows how to be any other way. She should give the girls a good stretch to their character!"

"Just the same, if she's so wealthy, why doesn't she hire professionals to do her work? And why is she paying the girls by giving them an old junk car?"

"I admit it's a little out of the ordinary, but I thought it might be a good opportunity for the girls to learn a few things about people and responsibility," Sam answered.

Mary sniffed and leaned over to check Sam's coffee, which didn't need refilling. "I still think that Holloway bunch is a little kooky. They've lived on that estate for over a hundred years like spiders in the center of a big web. I've heard of all the goings-on and rumors about their wild parties and such—of course, that was all long ago. No one outside high society ever knew anything about them. There was never anything in the newspapers."

"That's because they *owned* the newspapers. Now Mary, we know better than this. Rumors are just rumors and not worth the breath they travel on. Don't forget it was Mrs. Holloway who often gave me work when I was a drinking man. She knew nobody else would hire me. Many a meal put on this table was due to her kindness," Sam said. "Old Man Holloway used to hire my father and pay him well. When Pa got sick and lost his job at the block factory by the river, no one would give him work. For whatever reason, Holloway was kind to us. I guess I've sort of a soft spot for them."

Mary smiled. "I know that, Sam, and I don't mean to take that away from them. But when it's my daughters that are involved, I have to be suspicious."

Lien looked up from her book, her forehead creased. "Will Brenda and Amberley be all right?" Lien asked.

Mary and Sam looked at their youngest daughter, surprised. "Well, I guess little pitchers do have big ears!" Mary smiled. "Yes, sweetheart, I am sure they will be just fine. It's just that this is your sisters' first time working out of the house, and I'm not used to it. Honey, why don't you go upstairs and finish your homework in your room? Your father and I want to talk."

When Lien left the room, Sam set his coffee cup in the sink and stood at the kitchen door, looking across the field behind the post office.

"Who would have thought she was listening?" Mary said. "Sometimes I forget she has ears; she's so quiet and so small."

Sam nodded, but his mood was somber. "Mary, Lien is our daughter, just as if she was born to us, but I don't ever want her to forget who she is and where she came from. I thank the Lord for allowing us to have her, but we mustn't forget our responsibility to her real parents. They must have loved her very much. We can't pretend she has no past or that the events of that day never happened. She didn't start living the morning we found her out at your ma's farm."

"I know, Sam. I just want her to have a normal life, that's all."

"I do too, and she will have as normal a life as we can give her. I just don't want her to forget her heritage. She has a language and a people of her own that can't be taken from her. Someday I will explain to her about the flag of yellow and what the three red stripes mean. Soon I will let her visit the place in the hollow where her parents . . ."

"Sam, not too loudly!" Mary hushed.

"Not now, Mary, but one day soon. It's our responsibility."

* * *

"I don't think anybody's home," Amberley said.

"Maybe they don't hear us. Let me do it this time," Brenda said.

As she reached for the knocker, the huge oak door slowly swung open. There, standing motionless and silent, was a giant of a man dressed in a traditional butler's uniform. He stood rigid as a statue, facing the girls with his chin pointed forward. His eyes seemed to scan the horizon as if he were quite alone, and then, slowly and deliberately, he let them settle upon Amberley and Brenda.

The sudden appearance of such an austere figure was quite unnerving to the girls. Who would have thought there was such a person living in Sodus Township?

"May I help you?" the person said in a voice void of inflection.

"Yes, sir!" Amberley tremored. "We are Amberley and Brenda Bridges. We came to help Mrs. Holloway. She is expecting us."

The butler was silent for a moment, and then, slowly looking from one girl to the other, he uttered, "Dear me!", turned, and disappeared into the enormous house.

Brenda cleared her throat.

"Do you think if we made a run for it we could get onto the road before he comes back?" she asked. "He reminds me of Boris Karloff when he played Frankenstein's monster."

"Let's go!" Amberley whispered as they both turned to dash off the porch.

"Please don't go, ladies. Thelmy has just made a pot of tea," a voice said from behind them.

The girls stopped in their tracks and slowly turned about. There, standing in the doorway, was a rather tall, elegant lady who appeared to be in her fifties. She wore a cream-colored, lacy dress with a high collar. Her salt-and-pepper hair was fixed high upon her head. Her air was intimidating and masterful, but she had a kind face. She reminded Amberley of an old photograph she had seen of Grandma Andrews when she was a younger woman.

"I am Mrs. Katherine Humboldt Holloway. I know your father but haven't had the pleasure of meeting you. Won't you please come in?"

The girls slowly crossed the threshold, feeling as if they were entering another world. They were a little sheepish at first, embarrassed after being caught trying to slip away. Dad had given them a task and an opportunity, and they had almost failed before they got started. How could Dad ever have faced Mrs. Holloway again if they had run away?

"Theodore, please procure our refreshments for our young guests. We will be in the morning room," said Mrs. Holloway to the tall butler who appeared from the shadows to close the door.

The inside of the house was cool, dark, and cavernous. As their eyes adjusted to the light, they could see that the rooms were enormous. The ceilings were very high, the papered walls decorated with beautiful paintings and old photographs. The floors were of shiny hardwood with expensive European carpets laid out to the best advantage.

They were led down a long hallway, which suddenly burst into a bright, well-lighted room. The girls blinked at the sudden change in lighting. As they looked around, they noticed that the two outside walls were almost entirely made of clear glass panels, and the floor was covered with glazed brown tiles. The ceiling, which was also of clear glass, was very high to accommodate the seeming jungle of plants and trees growing out of the very floor. Singing and chirping in large airy cages near the treetops were canaries, parakeets, and several other varieties of tropical bird that Amberley did not recognize. This room was evidently the tower they had seen from the outside. The sight was so unexpected and beautiful that the girls were speechless.

Mrs. Holloway directed them to several comfortable chairs in the center of this man-made jungle.

"This is our aviary," she explained. "I really love it here, as did my late husband Harris. I can lose myself and forget that the gaiety and pomp of the old days have fleeted."

"It is the most beautiful thing I have ever seen. I could sit here for hours," Amberley said in awe.

"Thank you for your compliment, my dear! Ah, here is Theodore with our refreshments."

The tall butler never showed emotion but mechanically went about his duties and then stood at attention to be dismissed by Mrs. Holloway. At her command, he nodded and left the room. Amberley and Brenda couldn't help staring at him until his exit.

"Do not let Theodore frighten you, girls. He is really a most loyal and dedicated man, and I don't know what I would do without him. He has been with our family since my husband was a young man and then his father before him. He is ageless."

The girls silently took sips from their cups of tea but were too self-conscious to sample anything from the wonderful plate of fancy cookies that Mrs. Holloway called biscuits. Listening to the bubbling water and the canaries above them, mingled with the fragrance of tropical greenery, took their thoughts away.

Then with a crash, Brenda remembered that they had not come for a social engagement and returned her cup to the table. Amberley did likewise as Mrs. Holloway seemed to sense the mood changing. She tensed up and squeezed the arm of her chair as though she could make the girls stop moving.

"Ladies, I asked your father for your help because I have known him for many years. He has been in my home many times and has done excellent work. I heard that he had two lovely girls of high school age. I feel I can trust him, therefore I can trust you. I do not like strangers about my house. Do you understand?"

The girls looked at each other with wide eyes and then nodded together in the direction of Mrs. Holloway.

Mrs. Holloway pursed her lips and then sat back in her chair with a slight smile.

"I do not wish to appear mysterious, ladies, although I've been accused of that from time to time. I fear that I am a bit of a recluse and not accustomed to guests. Today I wish to just visit with you so that I may get to know you better. I want to know everything about you, including your hopes and dreams. What are your plans for the future? Who are your friends and your best friends and why? Tell me about your mother and father and the little Oriental girl you have adopted for a sister. I must know everything about you before we start. After that, we can begin next Saturday with the tasks at hand."

* * *

Later that evening, Amberley and Brenda discussed the strange conversation they'd had with Mrs. Holloway.

"It's as if she could read our minds," Amberley said, keeping her voice low. "She seemed to know what we were going to say before we answered."

"I know. It's kind of creepy," Brenda whispered. "How did she know about my real dad and the death of my mother? It's as if she has been a fly on the wall all our lives. And all those questions about Lien!"

"Well, it's important we get that car, so let's not say anything to the folks. So far there has been no harm done. Let's just see what happens next Saturday," Amberley said, turning off the little lamp on the table between their beds.

Five
Joe and the Farm

The sun had barely cleared the horizon when Sam set out east on Naomi Road to Shanghai. He balanced a cup of coffee on the dashboard and whistled to himself as he turned into the gravel driveway of the Schenkle farm. As he'd expected, Joe and his mother were already up, and he could smell bacon frying. Joe was coming from the barn, carrying a bucket of milk and a basket of eggs. He smiled when he saw Sam.

"Yer up early, sir," he said.

"I have to be up early to talk to you farmers," Sam chuckled.

Sam held up a bag of fresh-made doughnuts. The brown paper sack was still hot and steamy, stained and spotted from the hot oil the doughnuts had been fried in.

"Thank'ee, Mr. Bridges. An' please thank Mrs. Bridges fer me," Joe said.

"Brenda made these for you, Joe. She remembered you saying that you liked homemade doughnuts."

"I did, sir," Joe said, blushing at the mention of Brenda's name. "Nothin' better of a mornin' than hot fried doughnuts, lessen it's biscuits."

"Is your mother up?"

"Yes sir. An' I'd feel it an honor fer ya ta take breakfast with us, such as it is." Joe set the basket of eggs on the porch and reached out to shake Sam's hand.

"I'd be honored to sit breakfast with you, Joe. How is your ma?"

"Okay, I guess. She misses Pa somethin' fierce, and sometimes I kin hear her weepin' in the night for 'im. It 'bout tears my heart out."

"Mourning is a long process, Joe. But I suspect you are a great comfort to her," Sam said tenderly, patting Joe on the shoulder as they both walked into the kitchen together.

After breakfast, Sam and Joe sat on the back porch with their cups on their knees.

"Joe, can I ask you about your plans? What's on the agenda for your farm?"

"I plan on puttin' in soybeans, some corn and taters and such. Leastwise I'll have grain fer the cows 'n' hogs. I can grind muh own chicken mash."

"But how are you planning on making any cash?"

Joe thought for a bit. "I guess I'll carry on like Pa did. He had an egg route and sold vegetables and fruit to the stands on M140 and on out to Sister Lakes. I'll butcher a few chickens fer the neighbors and raise a hog or two. What little cash he made was made thataway."

Sam took a drink of coffee and paused. "Joe? I learned some things in the army. Maybe I can help you get organized. I have some ideas, and if your ma doesn't mind, we can sit down and talk about it."

Joe's eyes opened wide at Sam's offer. "I don't wanna bother ya, sir. You got yer own problems."

Sam smiled. "It would be a privilege to help you, Joe, and a favor to me. I never told you this before, but several years ago when I was at low ebb and out of work, someone would leave a bushel of potatoes or a chicken on my doorstep. Several times a month for a long time, food was left at our door this way. The person who left those things evidently knew I wouldn't take charity. Well, one morning, I looked out the window and your pa's old pickup truck was parked in the alley. I heard a noise on the back porch, and there was the biggest turkey I ever saw in a makeshift cage. I ran down the alley just in time to see your pa driving away. That's how I found out he had been leaving the food all along."

Joe leaned forward, holding his coffee cup with both hands, staring at the ground with a chuckle. "That was Pa all right. He did those kinda things, besides tryin' to keep this farm and family together and keepin' me from turnin' out like my uncles and cousins. So, you wuz the ones? I knew he was takin' food ta somebody, but he'd never tell me or Ma fer who."

"You see, Joe, I kind of owe your dad. Let me help."

"Sir, you'd never know how much I'd like that. Ma can cook and put up jars, but she don't know much about runnin' a farm. That wuz Pa's thing."

Then Joe paused. "I sure miss 'im, sir."

"I know you do, son," Sam said softly, as they both leaned back in their chairs to finish their coffee.

* * *

As the clock struck noon the following day, Mrs. Davison dismissed her class for lunch. Amberley was on her way to the picnic tables in the schoolyard to meet Brenda when Joe stopped her in the hallway.

"Amber, do ya think I could talk ta Brenda for a spell? Would that be okay with you?" he asked timidly.

"Sure, Joe." Amberley smiled. "Go on ahead."

Joe approached the wooden table where Brenda was seated alone. He noted how pretty she was with her shimmering black hair and the bloom of her face, and becoming instantly intimidated, he stopped to go the other way.

"Joe!" Brenda called out to him. "Joe, over here!"

Joe turned around, walked to Brenda's table, and stood silently opposite her.

She looked up at him with a smile. "Joe, please sit down. I want to speak with you."

Joe sat down, folded his hands, and looked at the table. "I wanted ta thank ya, Brenda, fer the doughnuts. They was good. No one but Ma ever fried me up doughnuts before."

"I'm glad you liked them, Joe."

Then Brenda grew serious and cleared her throat. "Joe, you remarked to me once about the difficulties you've had with your English and such. Well, would you be offended if I offered to help you with your spelling and grammar? I could work with you during recess and lunch hour."

For the first time, Joe looked into Brenda's eyes. "You'd do that fer me?"

"Sure, if you don't mind. I would love to help you any way I can. It would also be a help to me because I would like to teach English someday."

Joe hesitated, squinting his eyes in thought. He knew that he needed help, but the thought of the prettiest and smartest girl in school teaching him was intimidating. Still, the very thing that made him balk at her help attracted him too.

Brenda turned her head and stared thoughtfully at the old red brick building of River School. "You know, Joe, I remember how hard it was for me to learn. My mother died when I was very young, and my father didn't care if I was educated or not. I learned most of what I know by teaching myself and spending endless lonely hours at the library. I did all right, I guess, but I wished so many times that someone would have offered to help me and teach me. I thought perhaps you might like someone to help you."

"I would like that a whole lot," Joe smiled. "A whole lot."

"Then it's settled, Joe. We can start on Monday if that's agreeable."

Six
Brenda's Challenge

After his conversation with Sam, Joe grew excited about his farm for the first time, and he harbored a shining hope that it might all work out. In between school and his chores, he started to clean up the cluttered yard and paint the barn and the chicken coop. As he worked, he tried to talk courage into himself for a first lesson with Brenda.

The next evening after school, Sam came over again, and they sat down together and discussed all the possible ways the farm could make money.

"Now, Joe, I see that you have at least a hundred acres that are untilled. If you lease this land out to other farmers, it will give you money to help cover taxes. What corn and soybeans you grow for yourself will be feed for the livestock. You seem to have a pretty good established egg route. Why don't you ask your customers if they would be interested in buying a turkey from you in the fall or having you raise a pig for them to butcher? Remember, though, that turkeys have a tendency to get blackheads, so you will have to keep them up off the ground while they are poults and give them medicated feed."

Joe smiled. "I never thought uh these things, sir. I wish Pa was here. He woulda been excited too. He tried his best, but he never made much of anything around here."

"Well, Joe, you don't have a lot of any one thing, but you have a lot of little things. That's diversity, and let's see if we can make it work for you. The nice thing about diversity is that if one or two things fail, you still have all the rest. You know, if we can clean this place up, folks might want to come take a look. Especially the people from Chicago that come through here in the summertime. Shanghai, many years ago, was quite a resort area for people from Illinois."

"How would I start, Mr. Bridges?"

"I would be thinking about a nice fruit stand. I just happen to know a good carpenter who could help you with that," Sam said with a smile. "Besides fruit, you can sell honey from your hives, and maple syrup eventually. I noticed that you have hundreds of sugar maples in your woods."

Joe topped off Sam's coffee cup. "Pa liked to make syrup when he had th' time. I still have a few jars from last season."

"Your ma could help run the fruit stand. It would be good for her and for you. The trick is not to get in over your heads. Take it slow and grow into it."

When Sam left, Joe's head was swimming with the prospects of his future and what the farm might become. After supper, he decided to paint the old mailbox by the road. He looked through the cans of paint in the barn and found one half full of John Deere green. It was a happy color, and after finding a brush, he was soon laying on thick strokes of the bright green paint.

Joe quickly finished. He stood by, admiring his job, when he heard a pickup truck coming down the road. Thinking it might be Sam returning, he set down the paint and brush and wiped off his hands with an old rag. Joe turned with a smile on his face as the truck stopped in front of the mailbox.

"So, doing a bit of urban renewal, huh?"

It was Michael McGuinnes from the sawmill, leaning out his window with a look of mingled mockery and threat. "What's all the activity, Joe?"

Joe's smile instantly fled, and he stammered for an answer. "Mr. Bridges is helping me fix up the place."

McGuinnes let out a brittle laugh. "What's wrong with you, Joe? That old drunk don't know nothin' about farming. He's only done three things in his whole life: nail a few boards together, spend some time in the military, and drink a whole lotta whiskey. He's a fraud, and he'll take you down with him. Now if you're smart, you'll come to work for me. Think about it, Joe." With a thumbs up, McGuinnes drove off down Shanghai Road in a swirl of dust.

Joe felt the heat rise in his face as he picked up the can of paint and brush. After taking several steps, he threw the brush as hard as he could, striking the side of the barn. The brush hit hard, leaving a splatter of bright green on the freshly painted red wall.

* * *

True to her word, Brenda started teaching Joe the following Monday. She remained inside during her lunch hour to help him with his speech and grammar. It was more work than she had anticipated. Joe had apparently missed a lot of school, the result being that his formal education had been done with a lick and a promise. School had always been a secondary thing for the Schenkles, and Joe was often kept home to do farmwork and chores. He was promoted to the next grade as the desks became too small for him. Even so, Brenda believed that Joe was very smart and that she could help him.

Teaching Joe required a lot of patience, for he would quickly became frustrated and want to quit. He was accustomed to his teachers giving up on him, and he figured Brenda would eventually do the same. After several weeks, Brenda had had enough. Joe had gone to the cloakroom to get his lunch as a pretense and never returned. Brenda soon found him sitting on a swing, staring out across the horizon.

"You're never going to learn this way," she said.

"Sorry fer wastin' yer time, Brenda."

"Now say it correctly as I taught you!" Brenda said, letting the irritation show in her voice. "Cats and dogs are covered with 'fer'!"

"Aw, Brenda, fer goodness' sake!"

"I said say it right or don't talk to me! You're not stupid or dumb. You're just lazy, and everyone has always allowed you to give up on yourself. You are so full of excuses, Joe Schenkle, and I'm sick of it," Brenda fumed.

Instead of getting angry, Joe shook his head and smiled. "Brenda, what's the use? I'm too old ta learn and am never gonna amount ta anythin' anyway. Besides, I don't need grammar ta slop hogs."

Brenda stared at Joe, feeling her face go red. She couldn't believe what she was hearing. She stood with her hands on her hips and prepared to let him have it.

"If you had no intention of working with me, then why did you agree to it?"

"I guess I figgered you'd quit on me like ever'body else," Joe answered.

Brenda squinted her eyes. "If there's any quitting to be done around here, it will be you that does it. For your information, I know of a very successful man in history who taught himself to read and write and do math with the help of his wife. The only difference between you and that man is that he wasn't a quitter. Now make an effort to speak correctly and cooperate, or I . . . !"

Joe smiled but said nothing. Brenda let her mouth drop open and then quickly spun around on her heels and walked toward the schoolhouse.

"Brenda?" Joe said meekly.

Brenda stopped but didn't turn around.

"Sorry fer wastin' yer time, but—I've decided to quit school for good."

Without turning around, Brenda continued to walk toward the schoolhouse.

"I'll see you inside in two minutes," she said. "You may have time to waste, but I don't."

"Didn't you hear me?" Joe said loudly, standing up and turning around to face her. "I'm quittin! I can't do it all! It's either the farm or school."

Brenda abruptly stopped, turned around, and walked right up to Joe, nose to nose. She opened her mouth to speak but stopped. He cringed away, thinking she might be getting ready to punch him in the nose again. Brenda looked up into his bluish-gray eyes, smiled, and then reached down and took his hand in both of hers.

"Relax," she said, "I'm not going to hit you."

Then Brenda paused. "Joe, do you like me?"

He was shocked. "Yes," he stammered, trying to look away from her eyes to the ground.

"Joe?" she said. "I like you too, and I want to be your friend, and I guess this is the bottom line. I won't be with a quitter. If you quit now, you will do for it the rest of your life. If you want to be my friend, you can't be a quitter."

Brenda smiled at Joe, patted his hand, and then turned to walk back into the school. As he watched her walk away, Joe stared at the back of his hand.

"Brenda?" he shouted. "Brenda—I'll stay."

She stopped and smiled. "I'm glad to hear that, Joe. See you inside."

"But who was the man?" Joe shouted after her. "Ya know, the man you was talkin' about?"

"Do you mean the man who taught himself to read and write? The man whose wife helped him?"

"Yes!" Joe shouted.

Brenda paused. "Andrew Johnson—the seventeenth president of the United States," she answered, and with a smile of satisfaction, she quickly disappeared into the schoolhouse.

Seven

Lien Shows Them She Understands

Saturday morning, bright and early, Amberley and Brenda rose to start breakfast as a surprise for Ma. Lien heard them stirring and began to dress also.

"You don't need to get up, Lien," Brenda whispered. "Amber and I are just going to start breakfast."

"I will help you," she said.

"Sweetie, we really don't need your help. You can sleep in," Amberley said.

"I *will* help! This is my family too!" Lien shouted.

"Shush!" Amberley said, putting her finger up to her lips. "You'll wake Dad and Ma." Amberley and Brenda smiled at their little sister's emotional outburst.

"It is not funny! I am your sister, and it is my job to help too!" Lien said with such intensity that they thought she was going to begin crying. Amberley quickly put her arm around Lien and gave her a hug.

"You're right, Lien, this is your family too. You just want to help out and be a part of everything, don't you? Well, come on and get dressed. There's plenty of work to do, and on second thought, Brenda and I can't do it alone."

The girls made their way quietly down the stairs, pleased that they were up before their parents. It was just starting to get light outside, and rain was pattering against the windows.

"Now, let's not make any racket and wake up the folks," Brenda whispered. "Lien, you may start slicing the cornmeal mush, and I'll roll out the biscuits."

"I'll do the gravy and coffee," Amberley said.

Lien took the loaf pan of cornmeal mush from the refrigerator and carefully unmolded it on the cutting board. She sliced the loaf into uniform slices, coated them with flour, and put them into a pan of hot oil to fry.

Brenda mixed the dry ingredients of flour, salt, baking powder, and a touch of baking soda in a large bowl and cut in the shortening with a pastry knife. When the mixture was coarse and even with the consistency of cornmeal, she poured in enough cold buttermilk to make it into a thick dough. Brenda spread the dough out on a floured board, turned it over once and used an old metal drinking glass with a sharp edge to cut out the biscuits and place them on a sheet to bake.

Amberley cut up the fragrant, spicy sausage from Grandma Andrews's farm and put it on to fry. When it was well browned, she drained off most of the fat and sprinkled in several tablespoons of flour. When the mixture was brown and bubbling, Amberley slowly poured in cold milk and stirred until a rich gravy formed. It smelled like sage and made their mouths water. While the biscuits finished baking to their golden-brownness and the coffee percolated, Brenda turned the kitchen radio on very low.

"Here, Amber, listen to this. I just love Aaron Copland, don't you? This piece is called 'Hoedown.' It makes me wish I was a cowgirl."

"I know; it reminds me of being on the farm with the sweet-smelling hay, the bright summer sunshine, riding the horses . . . I wish I was there now, riding Gray back through the fields and the dark hollow."

Amberley suddenly stopped and put her hand over her mouth.

"Oh, Lien! I'm so sorry! Please forgive me, honey."

Lien looked puzzled. "Why are you sorry, Amber?"

Brenda smiled at Lien and touched her shoulder. "Amber didn't want you to be reminded of what happened on Grandma's farm, that's all."

Lien smiled and squeezed Brenda's hand while Amberley shot her a look—of all the family, Brenda was the least hesitant to mention Lien's past in her hearing.

"I know you have all been trying to protect me from what happened," Lien said. "My mother and father died out there because they loved me very much, and I think they would be very happy that I am now with you. Grandma's farm is a place of sadness, but is also a place of great joy. Soon, when I am ready, I will visit that place in the deep woods where my mother and father died to save me. It will make me think of Jesus giving Himself for me. Please do not be sad for me, my sisters."

Amberley and Brenda couldn't help getting moist eyes as they marveled at Lien's understanding. Suddenly, they heard sniffling from behind them and turned to see Ma standing in the doorway. She had apparently heard everything, and her eyes were full of tears.

"Suddenly, I love my three wonderful girls very much, who are apparently more mature than I have given them credit for," Ma said, wiping her tears with the sleeve of her housecoat.

"Good morning, Ma!" they chimed in unison.

"Surprise! Sit down to breakfast, Ma! Is Dad up?" Brenda asked.

"What is this? Breakfast already made? Now this is a treat, girls."

"And Lien helped! We couldn't have done it without her, Ma!" Amberley said.

Sam soon came through the door while drawing his comb through his hair. He seemed surprised at all the activity.

"I thought I was up early this morning, but it appears I'm late. Something smells awful good," he said.

"The girls were up before the chickens and made breakfast, Sam. Lien made the fried mush this morning," Mary said.

"Well, dish me up before I starve," he said as Lien beamed from ear to ear.

After the good breakfast was eaten and the plates cleared away, Sam and Mary sat at the table with their coffee.

"Lien, tell your Dad what you told your sisters this morning about Grandma's farm," Mary said.

Lien appeared a little embarrassed, and she looked to the girls for support.

"Go ahead, honey, tell Dad," Mary said. "I think it's important."

Lien looked at her father and began to speak to him in Vietnamese.

"None of that, now!" Mary said. "We are family, and you can speak well enough to express your thoughts in English. It is impolite to speak in another language when others cannot understand you. That's in the Bible."

Lien hesitated and then repeated the statement she had made to her sisters.

Sam leaned over and gave Lien a hug.

"Well, Mary, I guess we have been walking on eggshells unnecessarily. It seems that Lien is further out ahead of us than we thought."

Brenda went to the sink to begin washing the dishes, smiling to herself. A survivor herself, she'd never underestimated Lien's ability to deal with her past—but even she was touched by Lien's maturity and love for Jesus. Noting the pouring rain, she said, "I guess the driving lesson is off for today, huh Dad?" she said.

"Nonsense! People have to drive in the rain, don't they? That's the trouble with this world. Everyone is taught to function when the sun is shining and the skies are blue. We all need to know what to do when it rains, and that includes driving. Be ready, girls, in half an hour!" Sam said with his mischievous smile.

"Yes sir!" they said together and hurried up with their chores.

Amberley and Brenda did better on their second lesson but were still having problems synchronizing the clutch pedal and the gear shifter.

"It takes time and practice," Sam said. "One of these days soon, it will be as though a light switch has turned on. You'll master it yet. Just keep practicing. Next Saturday, I'll let you drive around the field without me in the truck."

Amberley and Brenda put on their raincoats after their lesson and began the walk to King's Landing. They had decided not to ride their bikes due to the weather.

"I wonder if she'll want to talk again. Katherine Humboldt Holloway! What a handle!" Brenda exclaimed.

"Dear me! Don't forget our Theo-dore!" said Amberley sarcastically. "I don't think he likes us at all. How did we ever get mixed up in this? I feel like a life-sized game piece on a Victorian board game."

"Well, she asked us to come for dinner today. That should prove interesting."

"To be sure, but what about all those questions last week? I am not convinced that we shouldn't have told the folks about it," Amberley said.

"Perhaps, but I don't think we have really kept anything from them. Mrs. Holloway is just eccentric and cautious about people who are beneath her station. Dad wouldn't have consented to this if he thought there was any danger," Brenda said. "Let's just try and get through it. And we definitely must do some work today. We can't keep going there just to keep her company."

The walk up to the big house didn't seem quite as intimidating as the previous Saturday. Theodore answered the door, and upon seeing them, responded with his usual utterance of "Dear me!", which was either an exclamation of surprise or disgust. They weren't sure which. They were promptly shown into the dining room where they were greeted by Mrs. Holloway.

"Good morning, ladies! Did your father drop you?"

"No, ma'am, we walked," Amberley said with a slight smile.

"Hmmm, that is certainly suggestive," Mrs. Holloway said, as if she was speaking to herself. "It does show an exhibition of character to walk all this way in the rain. Very good! Very good! Will you be seated?"

Mrs. Holloway behaved as if she had just worked out a long mathematical equation in her head and was exceptionally pleased with the answer.

The girls sat opposite one another at a long shiny walnut table. Mrs. Holloway sat at the very end and curtly rang a small bell. Almost instantly, Theodore appeared, wheeling in a narrow serving cart whereon sat a large silver soup tureen.

"I hope you like New England clam chowder. It was a favorite of my late husband Harris. Afterward, we will dine upon a wonderful version of trout amandine as the main course. It is a particular specialty of Thelmy's."

The air hung heavily with the atmosphere of the room. The girls avoided each other's eyes, afraid they might laugh or make some face that would give them away. That morning they had been two simple Sodus country girls eating biscuits and gravy. What a contrast to trout and clam chowder!

The girls carefully followed Mrs. Holloway's lead. As she picked up her silver soup spoon, the girls did the same. Amberley looked across the table at Brenda as she tasted her first spoonful of soup, self-conscious that she might be sipping too loudly.

Mrs. Holloway proved to be a master of small talk, and eventually the conversation drifted again to their sister Lien. She seemed so particularly interested in the details of Lien's life that Amberley showed her a recent photograph. Mrs. Holloway appeared to be captivated by the picture and held it cupped in her hand like a pocket watch.

Suddenly, Mrs. Holloway put the photograph down, excused herself, and left the room. Amberley leaned forward toward Brenda to whisper, "I hate eating soup in public! Am I too loud?"

"Yes! You sound like a cow pulling its foot out of a mud hole!" Brenda said without smiling. "Now quiet! Someone's coming!"

Theodore appeared from the shadows with his usual stiffness.

"Ladies, madame begs your pardon and regrets that she is unavoidably indisposed. She will not be requiring your assistance today. May I show you out?"

The girls were dumbstruck! They looked at each other, unsure of what to do. Had they offended Mrs. Holloway in some way? Had she taken ill?

Amberley was the first to rise from her chair. She stood for a moment and faced the looming figure of Theodore.

"Is Mrs. Holloway well? Have we done something to offend . . . ?"

Theodore cut off her last sentence with "This way, please!" He quickly turned about and led them to the front door. He stood in silence beside the gaping entrance, staring straight ahead and waiting for them to exit.

The girls buttoned up their raincoats on the front porch and heard the great oak door close behind them. It was now raining even harder than when they had first come. The nimbus clouds were low-hanging, dark, and fibrous and made the horizon appear as if it had been brushed and combed. The wind was only slight.

"Walking again," Brenda sighed.

"That is certainly suggestive," Amberley grumbled. "What in the world did she mean by that?"

The girls pulled up their hoods and began the long soggy walk back to Sodus. As they neared the sight of their house in the distance, the rain began to fall so hard that it hissed like sifting gravel, causing bubbles to churn on the mud puddles.

Amberley and Brenda said nothing as they entered the warm, well-lighted kitchen that was the heart of their dear home. Ma had been busy baking bread, and a half-dozen golden loaves were cooling on the table. She was relaxing in the living room, and when the girls came through the door, how happy they were to see her! The dark, bizarre world of Mrs. Holloway made their home suddenly seem so sweet and inviting.

"Why girls, you're certainly back early! And sopping wet!" Ma said.

Amberley and Brenda couldn't restrain themselves any longer. They quickly changed their dripping clothes, sat down next to Ma on either side, and told her all about Mrs. Holloway, Theodore, and the strange house in King's Landing.

"Well!" Ma said in shock and surprise. "I knew they were peculiar, but I didn't expect this. Do you mean she just left and never came back?"

"Yes, Ma!" Brenda said. "The situation changed like night to day. I can't think of what we might have done or said to offend her. Then she sent that awful Theodore to throw us out!"

"I don't ever want to go back there again!" said Amberley. "Not even if she offers to give us her Bentley!"

That evening they told their father the whole story.

"That certainly is an odd one," he said. "I know they are mighty eccentric over there, but this takes the cake!"

Eight
Thoughts Turn to Other Things

Nothing much was said about the incident with Mrs. Holloway during the following week. Sam told the girls it would be best if they stayed away from King's Landing and forgot about the car. Mrs. Holloway had severed communications with them without an explanation, and it was best to leave it at that.

Soon, memories of the Victorian house with its spectacular morning room and sinister butler began to fade in the light of summer's brightness. As the weeks passed, school let out and the prospect of vacation and rest filled the girls' hearts. Still, whenever they thought of September to come, Amberley and Brenda realized they were halfway through high school and still had no jobs.

The Bridges family had started a college fund as soon as they were able, but even so, there would only be enough money to start one of the girls. Amberley and Brenda had to find a way to earn enough for their first year of tuition, or one of them would have to stay home.

Along with her growing desire to become a teacher, Brenda had developed an interest in working with those who were given up as lost causes. Working with Joe seemed to awaken that desire. Having been told most of her life by her natural father that she was a mistake and of very little value, Brenda found herself determined to prove him wrong—about her and about every other disadvantaged person she could help. She prayed that God would somehow lead her in that direction and provide opportunities to help others.

Amberley wanted to become a writer, but she found it difficult to be serious about college. She still felt like a kid in high school. College seemed like a hundred years away. Perhaps, she thought, that was why Ma and her teachers sometimes called her a dreamer. Still, she knew that dreamers rarely accomplish much beyond their dreams, and she feared disappointing her parents if she didn't go to college.

"A writer still needs to be practical and know how to spell and understand rules of grammar and such," Ma said one day when the subject came up. "There is no free lunch, Amber. Anything you choose to do and be successful at takes preparation."

"I know, Ma, but how are we ever going to be able to afford college? There will only be enough money for one of us. Send Brenda!"

"God needs writers too!" Brenda said, as she sat in the living room with Ma and Amberley. "Someone needs to write books for children and adults that are clean and decent. I hate it when an author feels he must be vulgar or profane to spice up what is already a bad book to begin with. I hate suggestive talk! I guess it's because I grew up around so much of it. I want you, Amber, to write the books that my children are going to read some day."

Amberley sat silently for a moment.

"I want that too, Brenda. If God will let me, I'll write those books." She sighed, and followed the sigh with a grin. "I guess I'll even go to college!"

* * *

One Saturday afternoon, as Brenda finished working with Joe at the library, she closed her book and looked at him. "Joe, how are things going on the farm? I know Dad is enjoying building the fruit stand."

His face brightened at the bringing up of his favorite subject. "It's goin' great, Brenda. The stand is huge and will have 'lectricity for a freezer and fridge. Ma can't wait for it to be finished."

"That's great," Brenda said, and then she grew serious. "Joe, can I ask you a personal question?"

"Sure," he said with a smile.

"Did you or your family ever attend church?"

"I went to Bible school in the summer at the Lifegate Church on Union Road a few times, but that was years ago. Why you askin'?"

"Joe?" Brenda began, clearing her throat. "If something was to happen, God forbid, and you were to, well, die today, right now, where would you go?"

Joe thought a moment and quickly answered, "Hell!"

Brenda was shocked. "Joe, you believe you would go to hell? How do you know that?"

"I learned it at Bible school. I was born a sinner, an' Jesus wants ta forgive sinners and give them everlasting life. It says that right in the Bible." Joe paused. "I ain't asked Him to forgive me and be my Savior yet, so if I died right now, I would go straight to hell. Anyway, tha's what the Bible says."

Brenda was amazed at Joe's understanding. "Joe, that is true. Then why have you not done it?"

Joe paused and then quickly changed the subject. "Brenda, I gotta go now. I promised my uncle Will that I would help him change the starter on his old tractor. I'm late now as it is."

"Did I upset you?" Brenda asked softly.

"No, I'm jus' not ready to talk about it."

"I see." Brenda paused thoughtfully. "Are we still on for next Tuesday, then?" With that, Brenda and Joe parted, agreeing to continue meeting at the library.

Nine
The Fireman's Picnic

It was not yet nine o'clock, and Amberley could feel the humidity rising in the air. It tingled on her face when she stuck her head out the back door, and as the brassy sun rose above the treetops, the day promised to be uncomfortably warm. She was excited, though, because tomorrow was the Sodus Fireman's Picnic. It was held each summer to help raise money for supplies and equipment. Grandpa Andrews had been the fire chief before he died, so it had become traditional to hold the event by the river on the Andrews farm.

She looked forward to the big picnic. There would be Grandma's fried chicken, Ma's good potato salad, pies and coconut cake and all of the wonderful foods the other ladies would bring. There would be fishing in the river, and that night, fireworks in town behind the fire station. Best of all, Dad would be with them. As a child she had gone to the picnic with just her mother, but now Dad was a Christian, someone who need not be afraid to show his face in good company. She couldn't be happier.

That morning was also a special treat because Ma had told the girls they could take their breakfast outside and eat it at the wooden table in the backyard. Ma was working in the kitchen, baking pies for the picnic, and she needed the room to roll out the pie dough. It would soon be too hot in the kitchen to work, and she wanted to get it done. After breakfast, they would help her peel potatoes and shell eggs and cut them up for the potato salad tomorrow.

Sam had taken the day off work to help Joe with some projects on his farm, and Brenda rode along to help Maudie Schenkle with canning. Joe was happy to see her, and her presence and Sam's helped make his day go all too swiftly. As he went out to the barn to bring in another crate of canning jars, he noticed Michael McGuinnes's pickup truck parked down the road. Joe stopped and stood beside the big tree in the front yard to watch him. Mike had not noticed him, as he seemed to be intensely absorbed in watching Brenda as she sat on the back porch snapping string beans. Joe knew that Michael McGuinnes was a little strange, but this was too much. Joe set the crate down and began to walk in the truck's direction, but instantly, McGuinnes started up his engine and vanished down the dusty road. Joe said nothing to Sam or anyone else. He did not understand what McGuinnes's actions meant, but they were certainly unsettling.

* * *

It was the morning of the picnic, and Mary and the girls made ready to help set up the tables and food at Grandma Andrews's. Sam loaded his pickup truck with tables and chairs. Amberley was especially excited because she was entering a pecan pie in the cake and pie contest. Brenda had helped her, and Amberley was again surprised at how much her sister knew about cooking. She had learned everything she knew by reading library cookbooks —that, and poring over every page of an old cookbook her mother had left her when she died.

"Brenda, you're such a great cook," Amberley said as they sat at the table in front of the beautiful pie cooling on a rack. "You should open up your own bakery someday."

Brenda smiled. "Now, there's an idea."

"I'm serious, Brenda. You have a God-given talent. I could never cook or bake as well as you. Please come along to help me show off our pie," Amberley coaxed.

"You mean *your* pie, don't you?"

"No, I mean our pie, and don't you forget it."

Brenda had enjoying helping her sister with the pie but was reluctant to go to the picnic. She was not normally bashful, but her innate fear of failure and the disappointment it brought with it made her reluctant to be associated with the contest. Brenda had her natural father, Eltie Bickel, to thank for her fears, and she knew it. Still, they were hard to shake. She drew herself up. She would go to the picnic for Amberley's sake.

The afternoon was beautiful and sunny, with a cool breeze blowing off Lake Michigan. When the Bridges family arrived at the river, Brenda wondered if Joe would be there. He had teased the day before that he would not be coming, but she smiled when she saw his horse, Gypsy, tied up under a shady tree near the thick grass by the river.

At the top of the hill, the fire chief with his white chef's hat and blue-striped apron presided over smoky grills made from several old oil drums cut in half. The mouthwatering smells of roasted sausages and buttery ears of sweet corn wafted through the crowds of people steadily arriving in the parking area. The beautiful red Sodus fire truck with its polished chrome glistened brightly in the intense sunlight.

Sam and Joe and some of the men began to set up the tables and chairs in the shade near the top of the hill. When Sam was finished, he and Joe walked over to his truck and sat on the tailgate, away from the large crowd that was gathering. Most of the men had avoided speaking to him.

Not far away, Grandma Andrews was indeed the straw boss. She directed the ladies who had been appointed to decorate as they quickly laid out white paper from a large roll and festooned the tables with colorful decorations, promoting the firefighters' cause. She had been watching her son-in-law and could see that he was not comfortable. *This will never do,* she thought and walked over to where Mary was setting out the dishes and pans of potluck food.

"Daughter, I think you might want to speak with Sam. He's having a hard time of it."

Mary looked up at her husband and watched him brooding in silence as the men of the town avoided him. He was still a curiosity—the drunkard who had gotten religion. It was painful for her to see, and she wondered if Sam would ever be forgiven and accepted by those who only knew him as he had been before.

"Amber, perhaps you could stand watch over the dessert table. I noticed several of the children trying to stick their dirty little fingers into my lemon meringue," she said as she removed her oven mitts and apron and walked across to where the pickup truck was parked.

Amberley stood watch as Ma had asked and noticed that the contest judge had put a white ribbon on her pie—third place. She was surprised and happy. She knew that the first- and second-place ribbons would almost certainly go to the older ladies.

Mary walked up to where Sam, Joe, and Lien were seated on the tailgate.

Life in Old Sodus

"Joe, would you mind helping Brenda? Some of those boxes she has are very heavy."

"No, ma'am. I'd be glad ta."

"Sam, please come over and help me arrange the food so the people can dish up as they come by?" Mary asked tenderly, taking Sam by the hand.

"Sure," he answered with a smile, looking into Mary's sweet eyes.

"Lien, you help your father, okay?" Mary said. Lien smiled and nodded her head, but it was not a happy smile. She had somehow picked up on the unfriendliness toward Sam.

"Well, I see you made it," Brenda said to Joe with a smile as he approached her.

"You knew I'd be here," he said. "I brung . . . I mean I brought Gypsy along. You said you'd like to ride her."

"I can't wait, Joe. She is such a beautiful horse."

As Joe carried the boxes over to the serving tables, Brenda walked over to a tent set up on the other side of the hill for judging the quilts and other crafts. As she bent down to pick up another role of paper for the food tables, she heard two girls talking outside the tent. It was the voice of Vickie Taylor, one of her schoolmates, speaking with another girl she did not know.

"I don't know how she can stand to be seen with that rube. How embarrassing!" Vickie said, laughing.

"I know," the other girl said. "Doesn't he have anything else to wear besides bib overalls?"

"Well, there's no future in it. She certainly can't be thinking about getting serious with *that* guy," Vickie said, her voice fading as she and the other girl walked away.

Brenda peeked around the corner, watching the girls disappear into the crowd. It was obvious they were talking about her and Joe. She breathed out a heavy sigh and slowly made her way back to the serving area.

After dinner, the plates were cleared, and the adults talked over their coffee and dessert as the children played in the meadow below the hill. Suddenly, a bloodcurdling scream pierced the air. The casual, happy conversation among the adults hushed to a whisper as everyone looked around, trying to locate the source of the noise.

"Look, down there!" the fire chief said, pointing to the river. "Look at those kids!"

Below the hill near the river was a group of children who had been playing ball. Now, they were scattering in all directions like a covey of quail, leaving six-year-old Susie Washke standing alone like a frozen statue. She let out another scream as they watched.

"What's that on her face?" Mary shouted, holding her hand over her eyes to block out the glare of the sun.

"Get out of my way!" Sam shouted, as he climbed over the table where he was seated, sending plates and utensils flying everywhere. Sam ran down the hill with all his might. As he reached the screaming little girl, he reached out and scooped her up like a football, and without slowing down, he dove into the river.

"Bridges, have you lost your mind?" the fire chief shouted.

"My little baby! He's trying to drown my little girl!" Mrs. Washke cried out.

"What's that old drunk tryin' to do?" one man yelled.

"Just another burned-out Vietnam vet. He's probably high on Agent Orange," said another man, shaking his head in disgust. It was Michael McGuinnes. Amberley shot him a dirty look, but McGuinnes was only just picking up his tune. "Are we going to let that psycho drown that little girl?" he shouted, standing up on one of the tables and pointing in the direction of the river.

He and several of the men rushed down the hill after Sam. The river was swift and deep and not too warm. They could see him and the little girl being carried far downstream.

Oh, Sam! What have you done? Mary thought, putting her hands on both sides of her face.

As the men hurried down the hill to rescue the little girl from the crazy ex-Green Beret, they suddenly stopped and began shouting and jumping up and down, slapping their clothing and waving their arms wildly in the air. Frantically, they bolted one by one for the river and jumped in.

Meanwhile, Sam had finally climbed onto the riverbank several hundred yards below and was walking back with the little girl in his arms.

"Daddy!" Amberley shouted, as she started to run down the hill to meet him.

"Stop! Don't come any farther!" he yelled, motioning with his hand for her to go back. Amberley stopped in her tracks. As Sam walked to the top of the hill with the little girl, he kept a wide berth of the meadow where the children had been playing. As they came nearer, Mary noticed their faces and arms were peppered with red and white bumps.

"Oh, Sam!" Mary shouted. "What happened?"

"Yellow jackets," he said. "The ground below the hill is full of their nests. The kids disturbed them with their play. The only way I could get them off of little Susie was by jumping into the water."

He handed the little girl, who was whimpering softly, to her hysterical mother. Mrs. Washke reached out and held her tightly, with tears of relief streaming down her face.

"You should have a doctor look after her right away," Sam said. "Her face is a bit swollen."

"I'm so sorry, Mr. Bridges. Thank you for saving my little girl," Mrs. Washke whispered through her tears. "I just didn't know."

Sam just nodded and smiled.

"But how did *you* know?" Mary asked.

"I just knew," he said. "Training and experience, I guess."

"But Dad, how do you train for yellow jackets?" Amberley asked, reaching up to touch his face.

His voice grew solemn. "It happened before—in 'Nam. I saw a little boy get stung to death by hornets. But these weren't like the hornets we have here in Michigan. These were giant Asian hornets—as big as a man's finger, with a stinger a quarter of an inch long. I tried to brush the creepy little orange-faced monsters off him and roll him in the dirt, but it was no use. There was no river nearby, and we both got stung up pretty bad. One of the guys soaked us down with diesel fuel, but it was too late for the little boy. He stopped breathing and died in my arms."

"Oh, Daddy!" Amberley said, putting her arms around his waist. She glanced back with contempt at the would-be rescuers splashing in the chilly water of the St. Joseph River. These men had written her father off as a crazy, burned-out army vet, but now he was the hero. Some seemed to delight in keeping her father down. She felt a surge of victory over them.

"Let's get you home, Sam, so I can attend to your stings," Mary said, wrapping her arm around his.

Ten
A Worthwhile Investment

Hot August came, and with it the beginning of the tomato harvest. The sandy clay fields of Sodus were ablaze with shades of red, orange, pink, and green, representing the fruits in their various stages of ripeness. Armies of migrant workers moved rapidly through the fields, picking and sorting tomatoes ready for market from those on their way to the juice press. Men waited patiently, seated on their forklifts at the loading docks of the fruit exchange to offload the countless gray wooden boxes of deep red tomatoes, too ripe to stand the journey to the grocery store but fit to be pressed into thick, delicious juice.

Brenda was able to get a job at the fruit exchange, working in the stifling hot press room in the basement. It was a loud, frightening world with highways of noisy stainless-steel conveyer belts above and below, the hum of the steamy hot pasteurizer, and the jet-plane sound of the rotary press. Endless lines of steel cans and glass jars, like soldiers, marched their way to the filler bowls of scalding hot juice and then to the closing machines to be sealed with lids.

Brenda's job was to stand along a conveyer belt with dozens of other ladies, picking through the heaps of tender, sun-ripened tomatoes and removing any debris or unacceptable fruits before they were washed in cold water and plunged into the massive columns of the juice press. It was hot, miserable work, but she could stay as long as she liked. She often came back after supper and worked late into the evening. It was important to her that she earn every penny she could for college. Perhaps by the end of her senior year, she and Amberley might both be able to attend.

Amberley had been unable to find a job that summer, though she'd tried. She applied at several greenhouses along Highway M140, at the pickle factory in Hipps Hollow, and at the restaurant on Main Street in Eau Claire. Everything seemed to be taken. She felt guilty when she saw how hard Brenda worked and how exhausted she was each night when she came home. Amberley made sure that she did all of Brenda's chores as well as her own and helped Ma get supper on each night.

One Friday evening, Brenda came through the door for supper, soaked with perspiration and tomato juice.

"Brenda, are you sure you're not overdoing it? I don't want you to get sick," Ma said, putting down an old newspaper on the chair for Brenda to sit on.

"I'm okay, Ma. It won't be for much longer, and I like it that I'm helping to earn my own way."

Amberley was setting the plates on the table and looked pitifully at her sister. "Is there anything I can do for you, sis?"

"Oh, Amber, would you? I thought I was going to be off long before now and was to meet Joe at the library. He'll be there waiting for me, and I have no way of getting word to him," Brenda said, dishing her plate. "Tell him that I'm sorry, but I have to go back for a few hours after supper. I'll see him on Tuesday for sure."

* * *

Amberley inserted her front tire into the bike rack at the library and walked inside. Joe was seated at one of the rear tables, looking through a farming magazine.

"I hope you haven't been waiting long," she said with a smile.

"No, not long," Joe answered in surprise. "Your sister still workin'?"

"She didn't think she would be at it this late, but the foreman at the exchange asked everyone to come back for a late shift. It seems there's a bumper crop of tomatoes this year. Brenda asked me to come see you and give you her regrets. She is working so hard. It just puts me to shame!"

"I know," Joe said, shaking his head. "Wish I could help her."

Joe missed Brenda, and his disappointment showed. He quietly stared at his magazine.

"I'm sorry that I'm not Brenda, Joe," Amberley said softly. "But can I help you with your lessons? I don't mind if you don't."

"No, Amber. It's humilatin' enough to have Brenda teachin' me without the whole family in on it. I know you want to help, but with Brenda it's different, somehow. Did I hurt yer feelin's?"

"Not at all, Joe. I understand exactly," Amberley said, smiling and brushing her hair from her face.

"Don't get me wrong. Yer a peach an' all for wantin' to help."

"Say no more. I get it," Amberley said. "What are you reading?" Amberley had thought Joe was reading a magazine, but now she noticed a pamphlet tucked in among the pages.

Joe paused for a moment and then handed it to Amberley.

"Why, a Bible tract!" Amberley said in surprise. "*What Must I Do To Be Saved?* by Dr. John R. Rice. I've seen this before, Joe, and it's very good." She handed it back to him.

Joe paused and then spoke. "I was hopin' to get Brenda ta go over it with me today."

"Joe, may I go over it with you? I would love to. Has Brenda been talking to you about getting saved?"

"Yes, she asked me 'bout it early in the summer, but I guess I put her off. I think I am 'most ready to deal with it now. It's been eatin' at me for a long time."

Tenderly, Amberley took the little booklet and read through it with Joe. At the conclusion, she looked at him and spoke. "Joe, do you understand what we read? Do you want to ask Jesus to save you?"

"Yes," he answered, and together they bowed their heads. Joe prayed. "Lord Jesus, please hear me that I'm comin' to you this evenin' with all my heart, to ask you to forgive me my sins and to give me everlastin' life. Make me a Christian right now for Jesus' sake. Amen."

Joe opened his eyes and then looked up at Amberley. His face was flushed red, so intense had been his prayer.

"Do ya think that was enough? Do ya think He heard me?" he asked earnestly.

Amberley smiled, and she reached out and patted Joe's arm. "Joe, you don't have to beg the Lord Jesus to save you. All you have to do is ask Him, and He is ready and willing to do it. If you meant that prayer with all your heart, then Jesus heard you and accepted you, no strings attached. 'Him that cometh to me I will in no wise cast out,' Jesus said in His Word."

* * *

Later that night, as the family sat together in the living room, Amberley told the good news about Joe. Brenda had just come down from her bath and was seated next to Ma on the couch in her long robe.

"Oh, Amber, thank you so much for talking with Joe," she said, her face aglow and a tear escaping her eye. "I've always thought I would be the one to lead him to Christ, but I'm so happy it was you, sis. He told me earlier this summer that he understood the gospel but wasn't ready to be saved."

Dad put his newspaper down. "It seems that most of us don't get saved when we first hear the gospel. The Holy Spirit has to work in our hearts and show us our need of the Savior."

"I am so happy, Brenda, for both of you. If I was trading in the stock markets, I would say that Joe Schenkle is a worthwhile investment indeed," Ma said with a smile.

"What does that mean, Ma?" Brenda asked with a puzzled look.

"Never mind for now, sweetie. One day you'll know."

Eleven

The Final Straw

A dismal, chilly rain blew in sheets past a dim yellow street lamp and down the gutter in front of a nameless tavern on the east side of the airport in Benton Heights. It had been storming most of the day and into the evening, and nearly all the establishment's regular patrons were reluctant to venture forth and get soaked. It was late and near closing time, and only two cars and a pickup truck were left in the muddy parking lot of ruts and puddles.

Coming down the deserted street in the distance, a single pair of headlights shone brightly against the rain-soaked pavement. Barely slowing down, the car swung hard into the lot and skidded into a spot near the rear entrance of the building. The driver, wearing a baseball cap and hooded sweatshirt, quickly exited the vehicle and hurried to the dark, stale grotto of the bar, holding a newspaper over his head as an umbrella.

Once inside, he scrutinized the room to see who was there, and finding his mark, he walked to the back of the room as a desultory song played on the decades-old jukebox. The hooded figure pulled out a chair and sat down opposite a man seated against the wall in the shadows. The pair nodded to each other and sat in silence.

"Could you have found a sleazier place to meet?" the man with the hood spoke.

"I don't think it's anything you're not used to, McGuinnes. Have you figured out how we can do it?" asked the dark figure in the corner.

Michael McGuinnes removed his hood and pulled the zipper down on his jacket a few inches.

"I have it well planned, and I think the details will be to your liking. If we do it right, both of us will get what we want, including enough money to put us on easy street for the rest of our lives."

"You know, if we's ta get caught, we'll spend the rest of our lives in prison," the man in the shadows said.

"It's worth the risk. There are worse things than prison. Besides, this is Michigan. There is no death penalty here. And I've thought it over for a long time. Sam Bridges has been a thorn in my side since we were kids, and I hate him. He's stuck his nose into my affairs and humiliated me for the last time. He made a fool out of me in front of the whole town at the Fireman's Picnic and interfered with me hiring that stupid bumpkin Joe Schenkle. And because of Sam Bridges, I spent five years of my life in prison. I want him to pay," McGuinnes said, his voice getting angrier as he hit the table with his fist.

The man in the shadows chuckled.

"Don't worry, McGuinnes. We'll make him suffer the worst way you can make a man suffer: you take from him something that is precious. Something that can't be replaced. There's just one thing I'm worried 'bout, though. You say he used ta be in the Special Forces?"

"Don't give it a thought," McGuinnes laughed. "He's been a drunk ever since he got home from Vietnam. He's a shadow of what he was—that's if he ever was anything to begin with. Besides, he's got religion, and you know how those holy joes are. They don't believe in fightin' or revenge—no matter what. He can run away from yellow jackets, but that's about all the Green Beret that's left in him."

"Well, I'll leave the plannin' ta you. You set it up right, and we'll make Bridges pay. There's a lot of scores to settle with him on both sides, and I promise ya—we will break his heart for the rest of his life!" said the man in the shadows.

McGuinnes leaned forward. "I have some concerns of my own, though," he said. "Once we start this, there is no turning back, do ya hear? They say that blood is thicker than water. How do I know you won't get softhearted on me at the last minute?"

The stranger chuckled. "The only blood I have ever cared about is the blood flowin' through my own veins. I have no regard for anyone else and never have. That includes you, McGuinnes, if it ever comes down to it."

McGuinnes stood up to leave. "Then let's do it. Sooner or later, with constant watchin', the right time will present itself and we can begin. Be ready to go in a moment's notice. Do you understand?"

"I'll be waitin' to hear from you, day or night," the stranger said, throwing a five-dollar bill down on the table.

Twelve
Making Joe Understand

Brenda continued to work with Joe several times a week at the Sodus Library. He seemed to be making progress, and she even made an effort to improve his dress. Brenda feared that she might be too pushy, but if she was, Joe didn't seem to mind.

She told herself that she was just being a caring friend, but in her heart, she knew the truth. She was ashamed to be seen with him.

It was Thursday afternoon, and Brenda and Joe sat together at the library, sharing a soft drink.

"Bib overalls may be fine to slop the hogs, Joe, but they are not fitting for school or church, and especially not the library," Brenda told him. Underneath her teasing tone, she was dead serious.

"This is all I ever worn, Brenda. All the men in my family wear 'em. It's a Schenkle trademark," Joe said with a lighthearted smile.

"Well, I'll agree that it's a trademark, but I won't say for what," she said, not smiling.

As Brenda opened her English book to begin that day's lesson, the library door swung open, and Vickie Taylor walked in. She'd come in to drop off a book and didn't yet notice Brenda and Joe seated at the table in the back. Brenda was mortified, and without thinking, she quickly hung her head low, hoping she would not be recognized. Vickie came from a fairly well-to-do family and had been one of the popular girls at Sodus School. She was not a particular friend of Brenda's—actually, she had always intimidated her. Vickie quickly exited the library, never seeing Brenda or Joe. Brenda quickly composed herself and tried to continue the lesson as if nothing had happened.

Oh, what is wrong with me? Brenda thought. *Joe must have seen what I just did. What kind of a person am I?*

* * *

It was early September, and school had begun. The first morning's ride on their bikes to River School was warm, and the sisters were happy to see Mrs. Davison's smiling face once more. As the girls received their books and classes and settled in, they realized that they were now juniors and halfway through high school. It was frightening, but exhilarating too.

The girls had arrived home from school that afternoon and were up in their room, changing out of their good clothes. As Amberley closed the door to her closet, she caught a glimpse of herself in the mirror. She hadn't really noticed before, but she wasn't the little girl that she had always known. Her red hair was long and shiny, and her strawberry freckles accentuated the face of a young woman. She was growing up, and it seemed to have sneaked up on her without her knowing it.

Sooner than she wanted to admit, Amberley would have to make some important decisions about her future. She wanted to be a writer, but could one just graduate from college and then put out a shingle announcing to the world, "I am a writer. Inquire within"? She had to be able to support herself. And what if she met someone special? What kind of a man would marry a writer?

Brenda was also growing up. She had become tall and willowy and was very pretty with her shiny black hair and olive-brown complexion. Her real mother had been a Pottawatomi Indian from the Pokagon tribe in Cass County, and those roots showed on every inch of Brenda's face.

"I wish I was as pretty as you, Brenda," Amberley said, still looking in the mirror.

Brenda lifted her eyebrows in surprise. "I'm not pretty. I'm built like a lumberjack. You're the pretty one!"

"Brenda, you're beautiful! Don't you know that? Your hair is so shiny and black, and your skin just glows. I'm just a red-haired rag doll compared to you," Amberley laughed.

Brenda smiled. "Isn't it strange how we fail to see what others see? I was told so often by my father that I was ugly and worthless that I believed it was true." Her smile faltered. "I always thought he didn't love me because I wasn't pretty."

Brenda hung her head for a moment and then looked at her sister.

"I remember how frumpy he made me dress. He wouldn't allow me to fix up my hair or even wear a touch of perfume. Once, a farmer's wife brought over a bunch of pretty clothes and shoes to give me that had belonged to her daughter. Real nice things, you know. I was so happy because for once I could hold up my head in school. Pa came home later that night, drunk as usual, and threw a fit. He carried them all out and burned them in the ash can. He told me I was too ugly for such fine things and he didn't want me putting on airs." Then tears began to well up in Brenda's eyes. "He told me that nobody loved ugly people and that I should get used to it."

Amberley tenderly put her arms around her sister. "Sis, first off, you're beautiful. Second, it's just sad to put so much value on outward appearance. Let's change the subject. Every time you mention that man, it sends us all into a fit of depression. Those days are gone forever. And you *are* pretty . . . pretty enough that Joe Schenkle seems to notice you."

Brenda blushed, wiping a stray tear from her eye. "Isn't he a sight?" she chuckled. "I still remember the flowers he picked for me out of his woods. I had poison ivy for a week."

"I think he can't forget the attention you gave him the night he saved Ma," Amberley teased. "That's what started it all. Or maybe it was the day you rang his bell on the playground."

Brenda smiled. "I can't believe I did that. It's a wonder he speaks to me at all."

"You seem to have a way with guys. First it was little Billy Gussette from down the alleyway, and now it's Joe Schenkle," Amberley said.

"Stop it!" Brenda laughed. "Joe's not the same boy as the bully on the playground. He does have a good and tender heart, even though his grammar and appearance leave much to be desired." She sighed. "Especially his grammar."

"Dad says he comes from a family of roughnecks in Shanghai that have rarely ever darkened the door of a church. His kin have done everything from stealing cattle to burning barns. Wouldn't that be a charming family get-together for the holidays?" Amberley remarked.

"Look, sis! All I've said is that he is a nice guy, and I help him with his English, and you've got me married to him and living on a gravel road in Shanghai! Besides, his folks are different from his uncles and cousins."

Then Brenda paused, the smile fading from her face. "Joe asked me if I would go with him to the class party at the Ramona Skating Rink in Sister Lakes. I know it took him forever to get up the courage. I . . . I told him no. He looked so hurt."

"What reason did you give him, Brenda?" Amberley asked.

"I just told him that my folks didn't want me dating anyone yet, but I don't think he bought it."

"But Brenda, why didn't you just tell him the real reason?"

Brenda shook her head slightly and turned to look out the bedroom window.

"I guess I'm just a coward. I like Joe a lot—and I guess he knows it—but how can I tell him that I'm, well, embarrassed to be seen with him? I always thought I was somehow a purist at heart, above that kind of thing. I of all people have no right to judge others on their family backgrounds."

"You've got to talk to him, sis!" said Amberley. "He's not stupid, you know. He senses there's more to it than what you have told him."

"What do you mean? How do you know that?" Brenda asked.

"I . . . I mean that must be his impression," Amberley stammered.

"I suppose so," Brenda said. "I'm just waiting for the right time to talk to him. I don't want to—"

"Girls? I need help with supper. Your father will be home in half an hour," Ma shouted up the stairs. That ended the conversation for now.

* * *

The following Monday, Amberley and Brenda set out for school on their bikes as the balmy early autumn air teased them. Brenda pointed toward the sky, and they chuckled at the remains of Billy Gussette's kite caught in the power line by the township hall. Billy was a young boy and schoolmate of Lien's who lived down the alley.

The easterly wind blew them down the road as Brenda caught sight of Joe Schenkle walking ahead of them. Amberley glanced at Brenda as if to remind her of what she must do. Brenda knew she had to tell Joe the truth, even if it hurt him. She stopped and dismounted her bike to walk with him as Amberley waved and rode on ahead.

Brenda and Joe were quiet as they walked along. Joe reached over and took Brenda's bike and pushed it for her. He looked so pathetic. His bib overalls were terribly faded, and one of his pant legs was torn.

"Joe?" she finally began.

"Yeah, Brenda?"

"Joe, I need to set the record straight on a few things. The other day when I told you I couldn't go with you to Ramona because of my folks, well, that was only partially true."

"Ya don't need to explain," Joe said, holding up his hand.

"Joe, listen to me! I have done a very bad thing," Brenda said, her voice flaring louder as she spoke.

Joe remembered the fire in Brenda's eyes from the day they first met on the playground at Sodus School, and it showed on his face.

"I'm sorry, Joe," she said, modulating her voice. "The old Brenda dies hard. I just want you to hear me out. But Joe, when I tell you what I have to tell you, I'm afraid you will no longer want anything to do with me." Brenda reached out to stop the bike. "I have been ashamed of the way you look and the way you talk. I told you that my folks didn't want me to date, but that was only partially true. I used that as an excuse. And me teaching you—well, I really do want to help you. But I also thought that if I helped you with your grammar, I could make you acceptable. I've been ashamed of the way you dress and that you were part of that bunch in Shanghai."

Joe stood still, looking down at his feet and kicking at a small stone.

As Brenda quickly finished her speech, she thought, *There! I've said it. I've done my duty, and I'm off the hook. He's devastated, and now he will be hurt and walk away.* Then she thought, *What an arrogant little brat I am!*

But Joe only blinked at Brenda without expression, saying nothing. She frowned, confused. Didn't he get it?

"Joe, don't you understand? I've done a terrible thing to you. I am a horrible person. I don't blame you if you walk away right now. How can I ever expect you to forgive me?"

Joe paused and then spoke. "Brenda, I knew that you felt that way and don't blame ya one bit."

Brenda was surprised. "I don't understand. How could you know?"

"I could tell by the way ya looked around to see if anybody was watching when we wuz together. And besides, most of them things is true. That's why I wuz glad when you wanted to help me. I also knew by what your sister Amberley told me."

Brenda raised her eyebrows when she heard her sister's name.

"Amberley talked to you about this?" she asked in a low voice.

"Well, we did talk about it, but it was me that made her keep it secret."

Brenda put her fingers to her lips and paused. She remembered the intimate conversation of a few evenings ago, the tenderness and loyalty expressed between her and

Amberley as sisters. She couldn't believe that Amberley had let her go on and on about Joe without telling her that she had already spoken with him—and that they had been talking about her behind her back. The more she thought about it, the more hurt she became. Then the hurt blazed into anger.

Why, that little red-haired sneak! Wait until I get my hands on her! Brenda thought with sparks in her eyes.

Brenda excused herself from talking with Joe and rode her bike like a steam locomotive toward the schoolhouse. She charged down the hallway to her sister's homeroom and quietly peeked around the corner of the door. School had not yet started, and Amberley was chatting with Mrs. Davison.

"Amber, may I speak with you for a moment?" Brenda said with a false smile and a feigned sweetness.

Amberley excused herself and met Brenda in the cloakroom. Brenda slammed her books down on the cloakroom shelf.

"How dare you do this to me? I thought you were my sister!" Brenda roared.

Amberley caught her breath as though she'd been punched. "What did I do, Brenda?"

"How dare you lead me on, letting me go on the other night about Joe! Do you know how hard this was for me today? I was so humiliated! I thought we were more than just sisters. After our talk, I thought we were very special friends!"

Brenda fought back tears. She and Amberley had always been loyal to each other, but now she felt betrayed.

"Brenda, I am so sorry. I *am* your special friend, and I wouldn't hurt you or deceive you for anything. Please let me explain..."

Brenda cut her off. "There is nothing to explain! You had already spoken with Joe about how I felt, and you kept it from me. You deliberately let me agonize over telling him that I was ashamed to be seen with him, knowing that he already knew! How could you be so cavalier with my feelings and my confidence? How can I ever trust you again with the secrets of my heart!"

Amberley reached out to Brenda, but she just recoiled against the wall.

"Please, sis! Just listen to me for a second."

"Don't you call me 'sis'! I'm going home! I don't care what happens after this," Brenda shouted, pushing past Amberley to the door.

Then Amberley's eyes began to spark as she stood firm with her hands on her hips. "All right then, go!" she snapped back. "You won't listen to me or let me get a word in edgewise. Apparently our sisterhood doesn't mean much to you, either! And I'm glad I told Joe! At least one of us had the guts to be honest with him!"

Brenda was shocked. She had never heard Amberley talk that way before. The two sisters stared at each other, eye to eye, and then Amberley opened the door and went back into the classroom.

As Brenda turned to leave, the door seemed to open automatically as the knob pulled from her hand. There, standing tall in the doorway, was Joe. He had run all the way to school and was out of breath. Brenda tried to dart past him. "Excuse me, please!"

Joe stood his ground and refused to move, looking into her eyes.

"Brenda, this is not Amber's fault," he said, shaking his head. "I asked her to tell me how you felt and made her promise ta keep it secret."

"But why, Joe?"

"Well, when you offered to teach me, I figured you was jus bein' nice to me because I helped yer ma. It kinda hit me hard, though, when you wouldn't go to the skating rink with me. I thought that maybe Amberley could tell me why. I made her promise not tell you because I didn't want ya feelin' sorry for me, so you would feel like you had to go out with a dumb ol' hillbilly from Shanghai."

Brenda stood silently for a moment and then looked up at Joe with tears sparkling in her eyes.

"Oh, Joe! I don't think you're a dumb ol' anything. You're a fine, decent young man. What you did for Ma just opened my eyes to what a wonderful guy you really are. How could I not want to be your friend?"

"Well, Pa said that we was poor, and I had to miss a lot uh school to work on the farm. Because uh that, I can't read or write good. He told me that no modern girl might ever want me," he said, hanging his head. "Pa was jus' bein' honest."

Tears were streaming down Brenda's cheeks as she listened to Joe pathetically stammer and slaughter his English.

"Joe, I'm so sorry I hurt you."

"That's all right, Brenda," Joe said, smiling. "I know what I am, and that I'm not good enough for you, but you are so smart and beautiful that a guy has ta try. I can't help myself."

Brenda took Joe's big hand, already rough from his years of hard work on his father's farm, and tenderly touched it to her cheek. He lingered for a moment before pulling away.

"Now make up with yer sister," he said, smiling, and turned to walk the other way.

Brenda watched as the tall figure in bib overalls disappeared down the long corridor.

My gentle giant, she thought to herself.

Thirteen
A Fine Lady

It was Friday afternoon when Brenda and Amberley walked through the back door of the kitchen after a long week and another long, silent bike ride home from school. They were still not speaking, and they quickly separated upon entering the back door. Brenda went upstairs to her room, and Amberley set her books down on the table. Ma had gone shopping and Dad was still at work.

Amberley stood at the kitchen window with her arms folded behind her, wondering how long this game of silence was going to last. As she turned around, she noticed a letter propped up against the sugar bowl. It was addressed to Miss Amberley Bridges. *It must have come in the morning mail,* she thought and sat down to open it up.

The paper was fancy, the words handwritten with a fountain pen. It was an invitation for tea at the home of Mrs. Margaret Davison at 2 p.m. next Saturday afternoon.

Amberley smiled. *Mrs. Davison has kept her word. She has invited me to tea. But I certainly am not a fine lady,* she thought, remembering the last words Teacher had spoken to her over two years ago when she was still Miss Collins at Sodus School.

The back door opened, startling her. It was Ma with a bag of groceries in each arm. Amberley quickly jumped up, taking one of the bags that was about to fall.

"Thanks, sweetie. Where's Brenda?" Ma asked.

"I don't know. Upstairs in her room, I suppose," Amberley responded dryly, not looking up. She was sure Ma was aware that something was going on between her and Brenda, though she'd said nothing about it. How could she not notice? She and Brenda had been obviously avoiding each other and didn't speak a word during meals. Ma was evidently giving them time to work it out between themselves, but for how long?

"Ma, I found the letter from Mrs. Davison," she said, changing the subject. "It's an invitation to tea. I've never been invited to tea before."

Ma smiled. "Mrs. Davison asked me if it was all right to invite you, and I thought it would be grand. You will want to wear your new dress, of course, and your father said he would drop you off and pick you up."

"I'll be looking forward to it, Ma," Amberley said, helping her put away the groceries and start supper.

***

Mary had indeed noticed the little game being played between the girls and hoped it would soon mend. But after a weekend of ugly silence, with Amberley doing her homework at the kitchen table and Brenda in her room, she decided it had gone on long enough.

On Monday evening, Sam went back to work after supper to help Mr. Enkins put a water pump on one of his bulldozers. Lien sat in Sam's big chair reading a book. Amberley and Brenda had not spoken since coming home from school.

"Girls! I want to see you both in my sewing room," Mary said with a razor sharpness in her voice that they did not like to hear.

As Mary shut the door with a quick slam, the girls looked at each other eye to eye for the first time in several days. They filed into the room, where Mary ordered them to find a seat as she presided in her favorite sewing chair.

"Now I don't know what is going on between you two, and I'm not sure I want to know. You're not little girls anymore. The very idea, going about sulking like two hurt kittens! Whatever has caused this rift between you two must be soon mended, or when it does heal, it will leave an ugly scar. Do you both understand me?"

"Yes, Ma," Amberley said.

Brenda only looked at the floor.

"No answer, Brenda?" Mary asked, a bit surprised.

"Yes, ma'am," she said weakly but did not look up.

"I don't know what could have come between two sisters who obviously love each other very much, but it must end. Proverbs says 'a wounded spirit, who can bear?' You must decide within yourselves to end this nonsense, or your deep abiding love and friendship will never be the same."

Mary paused. "I want to tell you a story about Grandma Andrews and her sister Maureen. They had a falling-out over a boyfriend when they were teenagers and did not speak for months. When they finally made up, it was never the same again. Grandma says that each time they see each other, it is like two strangers meeting. Do you want that to happen to you?"

Mary looked for the effect of her words on their faces, but the story had apparently not made a dent. Brenda sat with her hands folded, looking at the floor. Amberley squirmed in her seat but likewise said nothing.

Finally, in disgust and disappointment, Mary stood up to leave the room. Before she opened the door, she turned and looked at the girls.

"I only hope that you do not let Lien see you acting this way. I don't understand it, and I know surely she will not," she said and closed the door hard behind her.

Brenda immediately stood up and left the room without speaking or looking at Amberley. In the distance,

Amberley heard the bedroom door slam. She thought about Ma's words and wondered if things would ever be the same between herself and Brenda.

Brenda sat at the blue wicker desk in her room, struggling to concentrate on her homework. She moved the curtain aside with her pencil and noticed that Dad had returned home. She knew she should be downstairs helping Ma do chores, and she missed greeting Dad with a hug and a kiss.

I just can't! she thought. *I just can't let it go and forget what that little sneak did to me!* Brenda felt like her heart was as hard as stone, and it frightened her. She knew that she had a wounded spirit, like the Bible said, and she was shocked at how far she had let it take her. And yet . . . somehow she still couldn't forgive.

"Brenda? Would you give me a hand?" Ma called up the stairs.

Brenda closed her book. *Oh, Lord!* she prayed. *How can I be so unforgiving?*

* * *

It was Saturday, and Amberley had spent the morning getting ready for the tea party with Mrs. Davison. She carefully dressed in front of the long mirror mounted on the back side of the bedroom door. Her new white dress with its lime-green floral pattern was beautiful against her red hair. The dress had been a gift—a birthday gift from Brenda. How she wished she could thank her right now and have her sister share in her joy—but their falling-out was serious and real. They were not little girls anymore, as Ma had said. The hurt they felt was grown-up hurt.

Amberley sighed and shook off thoughts of Brenda, pausing to take one last look before going downstairs. She put a finger to her chin and smiled. For the first time in her life she felt like a young lady. She didn't know if she was pretty. But she *felt* pretty, and that was all that mattered.

As Amberley descended the stairs, she could see Brenda seated in Ma's chair. They made eye contact for a moment, and then Brenda picked up a magazine and pretended to read. Amberley walked into the kitchen where her parents were seated at the table.

"How lovely you look, Amber," Mary said smiling. "I know you will have a nice time."

"I don't know if you should be seen with a bum like me," Sam chuckled. "You look beautiful, like your ma when I first met her." Sam looked at Mary, and her eyes sparkled at his.

"Oh, Daddy—thank you! That's so sweet of you," Amberley said, kissing him on the cheek. "But I will never look as pretty as Ma."

"Now enough of that," Mary smiled. "Many a war has started from such talk."

Sam held the door for his daughter as he carefully escorted her out to the truck. He opened the passenger door and held out his hand to help her in. As the truck rumbled down Naomi Road toward the edge of town, Amberley smiled. Perhaps someday she really would be a fine lady, as Teacher had said.

Mrs. Davison's house was little more than a four-roomed cottage near the end of River Road. It was white with green shutters and a roof covered with wooden shingles. Rose bushes were everywhere, and the beautiful, well-manicured lawn was green and healthy. Sam escorted Amberley to the front door and kissed her on the cheek.

"I'll be back to get you, sweetie. Have a nice time," he said, taking another look at how pretty she was. "You're mighty fetching, Amber. It looks like I'm going to have to start loading my shotgun to fend off the farmer boys."

"Thank you again, Daddy," she said, blushing.

Mrs. Davison opened the door and waved at Sam Bridges as he drove away.

"Have a seat, my dear. You look lovely." Amberley took a seat in the living room in front of a beautiful china tea service.

Margaret Davison looked beautiful in her long flowing dress, and Amberley could have easily forgotten that she was her teacher. As she poured hot tea into the petite cups, Amberley remembered how Teacher had been in those early days at Sodus School and how far she had come. After a few moments of small talk, Amberley felt so at ease that she decided to confide in her teacher.

"Mrs. Davison," she began, setting her cup down on the tray in front of her. "May I be bold and discuss a private matter with you?"

"Sure, honey. Ask away."

"I think that you are one of the wisest people I have ever known, and I need a bit of wisdom right now. I have a personal matter, and I need to speak to someone who is not involved in it."

Mrs. Davison smiled and set down her cup. "How may I help you, my dear?"

Amberley cleared her throat and related the entire story to Teacher, including how she had lashed back at Brenda that day in school.

Mrs. Davison smiled a little sadly. "I knew something had happened. You were so quiet when you came back into the room that day. Well, do you want my opinion or do you want advice?" she asked.

"Both," Amberley said, "but mostly advice."

"My opinion is that I think it was good that you spoke up to Brenda. Arguments are always bad, especially between siblings, but are pretty normal. I'm surprised this is the first one you two have had. I'm not going to go into who I think was right or wrong, but I'll bet that Brenda looks at you differently from now on. It's like getting nipped by your pet dog for the first time—finding out that he has a mind of his own and is capable of biting. But my advice is, this thing needs to end right now. I agree with your mother. The longer it festers, the more damage likely will be done. And I wouldn't be surprised if Brenda is also seeking a way to end it."

Fourteen
Brenda Gets a Visit

It was early Sunday morning, and Amberley awakened to find that Brenda had already dressed and was downstairs waiting to leave for church. Brenda would have never done that before without waking her first. Amberley was miserable.

As Amberley threw the covers back and sat up on the edge of her bed, she looked at her birthday dress draped over the back of the chair by the desk. She didn't feel like a fine lady just now. She got up, wrapped her flannel blanket about her, and sat down at her place by the window. The room was chilly, and she shivered as she watched the gray morning arise in an envelope of light fog.

Over Pipestone Road, she noticed a brown and gray kestrel, a small falcon about the size of a robin, perched on the power line above the coal yard. It was handsome as it sat motionless, surveying the fields along the railroad tracks for food. Then, spotting its prey, it began to bob its head up and down and flick its long tail in excitement. With a sudden burst of energy, it darted from its perch and hovered above the ground over the railroad tracks. For a few seconds, it beat its wings furiously and then stooped to the ground, snatching away in its talons a sparrow that was searching for seeds among the tiny shards of coal. Carrying its helpless victim to a nearby tree branch, it began to feed on the delicate fare. Amberley watched the feathers from the hapless bird float to the ground as the falcon began to pluck it apart. She was shocked by the sight, at the coldness and ease by which death could come.

Amberley thought about Mrs. Davison, who had become one of her heroes. She had turned her backslidden life around with God's help, made amends for it, and further prepared herself for her future. She had let no grass grow under her feet, and God had allowed her to meet a wonderful man.

Mrs. Davison was right. I shouldn't let Brenda push me around—but how can I think about my future with this between us? I can't. And I don't even want to. Ma and Teacher are right. This thing between me and Brenda can't be allowed to go on any longer.

Amberley broke down in tears and in prayer, determined that she would not let another day go by without asking the Lord's help and guidance for her future and somehow making amends with Brenda.

* * *

After church that morning, Sam and Mary and the girls started their short walk home. Brenda tugged her father's sleeve and spoke to him softly.

"Dad, may I stay behind for a bit? I want to speak with Pastor Mitchell."

"Sure, sweetie, if you want. Did you need us to wait for you?" he asked with a smile.

"No, sir. I will be along directly." And with that, Brenda returned to the church building to speak with Pastor Mitchell.

As Brenda waited patiently for Pastor to finish shaking hands and saying good-bye to the line of people by the door, she thought about what she was going to say. It had only been several years ago that her life had been in a state of hopelessness. The Lord had used Amberley to intervene when she found Brenda crying at the swings in the schoolyard after she had been beaten up by her drunken father. How mean Brenda had been to her—yet Amberley had still been willing to show her compassion and share the love of Christ.

My little sister! she thought. *Oh Lord, please forgive me!*

As the last person left the building, Brenda timidly approached the pastor.

"Pastor Mitchell, may I speak with you?"

"Why yes, Brenda," he said, motioning for her to sit down. "How may I help you?"

Brenda explained the whole story to Pastor, and when she was through, Pastor Mitchell smiled.

"Your mother was right, Brenda. Proverbs 18:14 reads, 'The spirit of a man will sustain his infirmity; but a wounded spirit who can bear?' Hurt feelings are serious business. When we perceive that we have been unjustly treated, our love and regard for someone can be turned into something like hate. We sulk, we pout, we avoid, and I am sorry to say, we act like little children."

Brenda looked away in conviction when she heard the last statement.

"Let me give you another verse, Brenda. In fact, it is the verse just before the one your mother quoted. Proverbs 18:13: 'He that answereth a matter before he heareth it, it is folly and shame unto him.' You told me that Amberley pleaded with you several times to let her explain, and you wouldn't let her. You owed it to her and to everyone else to get the story straight before pronouncing judgment. Now she is angry because of that, and the original issue for which you were troubled is clouded.

"I am not going to tell you that your feelings are not real or that you didn't have a good reason to be upset. But I will say this, if Amberley was wrong, she is still your sister and your best friend. You need to forgive her and let her back in and pray that no permanent damage has been done. I purposed a long time ago that I would never let anything come between myself and those I love, especially my own family. What started out as an unfortunate misunderstanding has now become a game between you two. I would venture to guess that Amberley is about as tired of playing it as you are. In the end, between two sisters, it doesn't really matter who was at fault, does it?"

Brenda thanked the pastor for his wise counsel, and they prayed together that God would restore the love and friendship between herself and her sister.

As Brenda began her lonely walk home, she observed that the streets were almost deserted. The warm autumn sun had come out and burned off the thick mist of that morning, revealing bright smatterings of red and orange and yellow among the sugar maples along Naomi Road. Brenda remembered the first time she had walked this way with Amberley and how she had felt when Ma had held her tightly in her arms as if she was one of her own. She picked up her step, anxious to walk through the back door of her warm little world with Dad and Ma and Lien and Amberley again.

Suddenly, she noticed a large blue sedan, driven by a woman, drive slowly by and then turn around and come back. As it stopped a little ahead of her, the driver's window rolled down and a middle-aged woman with blonde hair called out to her, "Brenda?"

"Yes, ma'am?" Brenda answered, not recognizing the woman or the car.

"Oh, thank God! I have been looking for you. There has been a terrible emergency at your house. I'm afraid it's your sister Amberley!"

Brenda felt as if she had been punched in the stomach. What could have happened in just a few short moments to her sister? If Amberley was hurt or worse, she wouldn't be able to bear it.

"Is she hurt? What's wrong?" Brenda shouted.

"Quickly! Get in the back seat and I'll take you to her."

Out of reflex, Brenda opened the door and slid into the seat. Before she could close it, the car quickly turned about and sped away eastward out of town. The momentum threw her to the opposite side of the car, against the person who sat facing the window. Almost nose to nose with her, the stranger turned slowly, removing his sunglasses with a grin. Brenda sucked in a gulp of air and felt the hair on her scalp prickle.

"What's the matter, worthless? Ain't ya happy to see yer old pa?"

It was Eltie Bickel, her real father, who had been ordered by a judge two years ago to leave the state and never return. The same father who had never let a day pass without reminding her that she was of no more value to him than a stick of kindling wood. In an instant of time, all of the several years of love and kindness spent living with the Bridges family seemed to vanish. Her eyes remained fastened on him.

"So you got nothin' to say? Well, you said plenty to that sheriff and that judge. Did you really think you saw the last uh me? Huh?" said Bickel, working himself up into a heat. "We'll see if the cat's got your tongue, all right, before I'm through with you!"

"Why are you doing this? What do you want with me?" Brenda said, trying to keep herself from fainting.

"Well now, I thought you'd like to come an' live with yer old pa again in the South. I kinda miss that gov'mint check you brung me. Or I might could sell ya to a work camp. I know a couple that would pay several thousand dollars or more for a good strong field hand. And then when they're done with you, they'll make sure there is no evidence for the police to find."

Brenda had heard all her life about migrant workers being enslaved across the south in "stoop labor" camps, used to pick fruits and vegetables, kept in tow by threats, beatings, and other more terrible forms of intimidation. She had never dreamed that something like that might become her destiny.

Brenda was horrified at what was happening. Her eyes flickered from left to right, trying to figure a way of escape. Bickel seemed to read her mind, and he opened his faded brown jacket to reveal the butt of a pistol tucked in his belt. Brenda looked from her father's face to the gun and then back again. Then, as if by an unspoken command, she slowly eased back against the seat, inert and helpless.

Life in Old Sodus

Brenda's mind raced in desperation, trying to find the answer to an unanswerable problem as the car sped away, faster and faster, from her beloved home and family in Sodus. Then suddenly, she remembered the Lord.

Oh Lord, what a horrible trap I'm in! she cried out in her heart. *I pray that You might save me out of this trouble, but if not, help me not to make You ashamed of me. I do put my life and my all in Your hands.*

Then Brenda turned to her father.

"Daddy, please don't do this. I know you never loved me, and I don't know if you ever loved Mom. But please do what's right for once. Don't shame me, your own daughter," she said, fighting back tears.

"Them police and judges had no right to take ya from me. Yer *my* propity!" he shouted angrily. "You're just a half-breed daughter of a squaw I was unlucky enough to meet up with. If it wasn't for the welfare checks you brung me, I would have left you for dead years ago."

The vile, poisonous words her father spoke pierced through Brenda's soul like a sword. The blonde woman who drove the car kept glancing back at her, and Brenda was surprised to see a look of pity and empathy on her face. Who she was and what she had to do with this, Brenda did not know. She gathered her courage to speak again.

"Daddy, I am a Christian now and have asked God to help me. I am afraid that He might . . ." Brenda paused, trembling.

"Might what?" Bickel shouted.

"He might hurt you if you don't let me go," Brenda blurted out, not believing her own boldness.

"So ya think God's gonna hurt me, huh?" he said with a laughing sneer. "I heard ya got religion livin' with that family. Well, ya better keep prayin'. You're goin' to need God and the Angel Gabriel before this is over."

* * *

Mary had cleared the dinner table but left a place for Brenda. With a frown, she noticed the time—almost two hours since they had left her to speak with Pastor, and Brenda was still not home.

"Sam? Brenda has not come home. Would you walk up the street and see what's keeping her?"

"Sure, Mary," Sam said, putting down the newspaper and looking at his watch.

Sam walked to the church building. It was locked. The parking lot was empty, so he went next door and knocked on the door of the parsonage. Pastor Mitchell was surprised to see him.

"Why no, Sam. Brenda left almost an hour ago. She should have been home by now," Pastor said.

Something was wrong. Brenda would not go anywhere without telling them first. As Sam hurried down the street back home, he noticed Billy Gussette playing

Life in Old Sodus

catch at the little pie-shaped park in the center of town with a friend.

"Have you boys seen Brenda?" he asked.

"Yes, sir," Billy answered. "I saw her talking to a lady in a blue car. She got in and they drove away."

"Which way, Billy?"

Billy pointed down Naomi Road, eastward out of town. Sam saw Officer Moore, the part-time Sodus policeman, parked at the gas station next to the coal yard. He waved at him to get his attention.

"John, I think my daughter Brenda might have been kidnapped!"

Soon a bulletin was put out, and every available policeman was out looking for the blue car and for Brenda. Sam and Mr. Enkins also went out, carefully searching every path and back road around Sodus, but sadly returned without success.

Amberley was in shock, not knowing what to say. She had envisioned herself and Brenda making up that afternoon, perhaps in tears, making vows to one another to never fight or do anything to sacrifice their unique friendship for anything or anybody. But now, in a wisp of time, Brenda was gone—and Amberley might never see her alive again.

Several hours later, as the sun began to hang low in the west, the Bridges family sat quietly in their living room, waiting for news. The phone rang.

"It's the sheriff, Sam," Mary said, handing the receiver to her husband.

Sam took the phone and turned away from his family.

"Sam? Sheriff Warner here. We have found a wrecked car in the deep ravine near the first curve in Hipps Hollow. We don't know how long it's been there . . . or even if it's the right car," he said as kindly as possible.

"But is there anyone inside?" Sam asked.

The sheriff paused. "Sam, I think you should prepare for the worst. The car is on its top and badly smashed. We can't tell if anyone is inside until we get it pulled back up the hill. If anyone is in that car, I doubt if they could have survived."

Sam put the phone down and turned to his little family, who were standing next to him. Sam reached out and put his arms around his wife and daughters. They looked into his face, waiting for him to tell them the news they dreaded to hear.

"I'm not going to mince words. They have found a badly damaged car in the hollow." Sam paused to swallow. "He believes that if anyone is in the car—they are all dead!"

Fifteen
Facing Their Worst Fears

The darkness was settling in Hipps Hollow as several police cars and a Sodus fire truck positioned their spotlights on the wreckage below the hill. Two tow trucks were needed to pull the heavy car up the steep side of the ravine. As the tow cables stretched and strained under their load, the dripping car dug hard into the dirt and grass.

Sam stood silently by, watching the sad work below, as the girls and Mary kept vigil in the back of the sheriff's patrol car.

To Amberley, the scene was surreal. She could very well have been a bird perched on a high branch watching it all unfold. The thought that her dear sister might be in that horrible wreckage, crushed and dead, was too much for her to process. She wanted to look away but couldn't. She had to be there with her mother and everyone else, like the young woman she was becoming and not a child.

As Sam waited patiently for the wrecked car to be brought up the hill, he thought he heard the unmistakable *clop clop* of horse's hooves off in the distance. He turned to look, and against the orange streaks in the western sky, he could dimly see the lone figure of a man on a horse, approaching from Hillandale Road. The man sat tall in his saddle and was carrying a lantern. As he came nearer, Sam could see the occasional spark cast off the iron of the horse's shoes. The rider approached the breast of the hill, and Sam could see that it was Joe Schenkle.

Sam smiled faintly. The sight brought back memories of the night Joe had rescued Mary from the wreckage of the old pickup truck in a blinding snowstorm, not far from this very place. He had brought her home, safe and sound, wrapped in blankets in his horse-drawn wagon, carrying the same faded red lantern. Perhaps Joe's presence now was a harbinger that Brenda would be all right.

Joe smiled a feeble smile and nodded at Sam, but said nothing.

The mass of crushed and twisted metal was finally pulled to the top of the hill, coming to rest on the shoulder with a crashing thud. As another wrecker pulled it right-side up, the awaiting workman began to cut and pry at the crushed roof. With the jagged metal finally cut through, several of the men leveraged the roof free. They flopped it over, and it thumped onto the pavement.

Sam and Joe hurried to the scene as Mary listened intently at the car window. Amberley and Lien held their breaths in expectation. In a few moments, she could hear a deputy talking to Sheriff Warner in a business-like tone.

"Well, I didn't expect this, sir!"

Mary turned from the window and buried her face in Amberley's shoulder. *Could Brenda really be dead? Who could have tricked her into getting into that car?*

Sam hurried back to the sheriff's car and opened the back door.

"Mary, listen to me! You are not going to believe it, but the car is empty! It matches the description of the one Brenda was supposed to be in, but no one is in it."

Mary turned and brushed the hair from her face and the tears from her eyes.

"But where is she? Where is our Brenda?" she shouted.

* * *

It was late in the evening, and Mary sat on the couch in Sam's arms. She had finally dozed off, and Sam was careful not to awaken her. Amberley and Lien sat at the kitchen table working on homework, but neither could concentrate. They were awaiting news of Brenda. The sheriff had said he would call them at about ten o'clock either way.

The kitchen clock ticked away as Sam dozed next to his wife. The phone suddenly rang. Mary quickly sat up, wiping her eyes as the girls turned to look at their father.

It must be the sheriff! Sam thought, and jumped up to answer it.

"Mister Bridges?" the female voice said. "Sam Bridges?"

"Speaking," Sam answered.

"There is an envelope tucked under the windshield wiper of your truck. It's about Brenda. Do exactly as the letter says."

"Who is this?" Sam shouted, but it was too late. He heard the click of the receiver.

Dashing out the door to his pickup truck, Sam snatched the envelope off his windshield and brought it back inside. Carefully, he cut it open with a sharp knife and read the letter inside. It was short and to the point.

> If you want to see your daughter alive again, it will cost you $250,000. I know you can get it from that rich widow friend of yours, so don't say you don't have it. You have forty-eight hours. You will be contacted with further instructions. Let the money be in all tens and twenties.

"What is it, Sam? Mary asked.

Sam didn't answer, but quickly picked up the phone and dialed.

"Sheriff? Sam Bridges here. I just received a ransom note for Brenda."

Life in Old Sodus

Mary sat down hard in a kitchen chair, and Amberley and Lien rushed to her side.

Sam hung up the phone and sat down beside his wife.

"Who could have done this, Sam? What are we going to do?" Mary said as Amberley wiped her face with a cool cloth.

"The sheriff is on his way over, Mary, and I guess I need to go see Mrs. Holloway." He squared his jaw. "You will never know how hard it is for me to ask her for money, but I would crawl on my belly for Brenda!"

After the sheriff left with the ransom note, Sam called Mrs. Holloway and asked if he might speak with her. He briefly explained the circumstances of the kidnapping, and she told him to come right over. He threw on his jacket and went out to the alley to his pickup truck. Sam heard the door slam behind him and turned to look. It was Amberley.

"Daddy, please let me go with you to Mrs. Holloway's. Maybe I can keep you company," she said, taking his arm. Sam smiled and nodded at his daughter, who quickly climbed into the truck with him.

Sixteen
Mrs. Holloway Has a Secret

It was already dark when Sam and Amberley pulled up in front of Mrs. Holloway's estate in King's Landing. The porch lights were blazing as Sam parked his truck, and Theodore was standing at the heavy oak door when they walked up the few steps. The tall butler, expressionless as always, asked them to follow him and led them deep into the bowels of the big house.

Theodore took them up a flight of stairs and down a long corridor into a large, cold room. The chamber was large and dark and had a sweet, musty odor like the stale yellow leaves of a very old book. The woodwork was dull, and the walnut bed frame split and cracked from exposure to many years of dry, unheated air. The curtains and bedspread were dusty and faded, and the old-fashioned wallpaper was loose and beginning to peel in wide strips.

The dusty shade on the window was yellow, stained from age and years of neglect.

A long row of dolls in assorted sizes sat along the bed against the pillows. Their faces were almost indiscernible in a heavy coating of dust and cobwebs. Amberley shivered at the bizarre sight.

Seated at a small, dusty writing desk near the corner was Mrs. Holloway. She bid them to enter.

"The room is quite dark and dusty, I know, but please have a seat," she said, pointing to two chairs that Theodore had set out for them.

Mrs. Holloway nodded at the tall butler, and he hastily departed.

"Thank you, ma'am," Sam said, looking around him at the uninviting room. He had seen odd behavior from the Holloways before, but this—this was oppressively strange.

Mrs. Holloway sat still for several moments before speaking.

"Mr. Bridges, I have already called my banker, and the money will be ready when you need it, and in the denominations you requested."

Sam swallowed as he searched for words. What did one say in a situation like this? He had just asked an almost total stranger for a quarter of a million dollars, and she had effortlessly made it available to him. It was just a loan, he tried to convince himself. *What a strange word—loan!* He would not be able to pay this loan back if he had two lifetimes to do it.

"Mrs. Holloway, I have no words to thank you. This is the most difficult thing I have ever had to do, to come to you like this with hat in hand. You and your family have been kind to us over the years, but I never dreamed that I would ever have to do this. I know you don't understand how we feel, but . . ."

"Sam," Mrs. Holloway said, interrupting him. "May I call you Sam? Besides the obvious dust and the ancient wallpaper, does this room seem unusual to you?"

Sam was surprised by her sudden familiarity. He thought the room very unusual indeed. It seemed to have been a little girl's room—but why so neglected?

"Yes, ma'am. Was this your daughter's room?" he asked softly.

"This room has been closed since my late husband Harris nailed it shut in a sudden fit of heartbroken sorrow many years ago. I have not dared to open it since, because it represents my terrible folly and selfish past. Tonight I thought I should face that past."

Mrs. Holloway stood and walked to the window, pulling the cord on the mildew-stained shade. It instantly rolled up with a dusty flutter, sending a plume of dust into the air.

"Yes, I am very eccentric, I know," she began. "A rich old widow living in a big house ten times larger than she needs with an odd duck for a butler. I know what people say about us, and much of it is true."

Mrs. Holloway turned to Amberley. "My dear, you are probably wondering why I left you so abruptly after dinner and had Theodore show you out. It was very rude of me, and I apologize. Perhaps you will understand, and forgive and pity me, once I explain."

Mrs. Holloway held a handkerchief to her eyes to stem the flowing moisture as she told her strange story.

"My husband, a brave and noble soul, was a captain in the army during the Korean War. He was not like the rest of his family, who isolated themselves and dismissed the conflict as simply 'Mr. Truman's War.' He enjoyed military life and all the adventure and felt true compassion for the Korean people.

"Harris had trained as a commando and was a specialist with all kinds of weapons, an expert in survival. He told me of many of the brave and daring exploits of his special unit, and I couldn't help being proud of him.

"We had been married for only six months when his unit was shipped overseas to the war. I was very proud that he was serving, not necessarily because I was a patriot, but because it engendered empathy from my friends and gave me a social edge. My husband's father offered to use his influence and get his orders changed, but Harris refused.

"Harris served bravely and was even wounded while attempting to rescue several men taken prisoner during a battle. He was awarded the Silver Star and the Purple Heart. I was the envy of our exclusive circle of friends. I was almost disappointed when he was scheduled to come home, because now the sympathy I was receiving would certainly wane. The day finally came, and I met him at the airport. All of my family and friends were there, including our parents. What a proud and glorious day it was—for me, that is!"

Mrs. Holloway turned and handed Sam a small wooden frame, displaying the medals belonging to Captain Harris Holloway. She smiled and continued her story, still standing.

"The door opened on the airplane, and I saw my hero husband standing there. He had lost a lot of weight but was still handsome in his uniform. As he came into view from across the tarmac, I noticed that he had his duffel bag slung over one arm and a tiny little Korean orphan girl in the other.

"I was shocked and then embarrassed. How could he have done this to me? Instead of giving my brave husband a hero's welcome, I did not try to hide my disgust and anger. I turned around and went to sit in the limousine. Everyone just stood there with gaping mouths, not sure what to do or say." She paused for a moment and swept the peculiar room with her eyes. Her voice shook a little.

"Before I was married, the doctor told me that I would never be able to have children of my own. I told this to

Harris, and he married me anyway because he loved me so. I'll never forget his face when he walked off that plane. He told me that he had brought us a little daughter to love and care for."

Mrs. Holloway sat down again and wept hard for a few moments. Sam and Amberley stole a glance in their discomfort at hearing such intimate details of the Holloways' lives.

Mrs. Holloway gathered control and began again. "Little Soon-ei was a beautiful girl. Your little Vietnamese sister reminds me a lot of her. That is why I couldn't come back to the table after you showed me her photograph. It struck such a painful chord of guilt in my heart. I learned to love the little girl, but I was ashamed that she was Korean. I was also bitter in my heart against God because He wouldn't allow me to have children of my own.

"Soon-ei was only six years old. I kept her out of sight and had her privately tutored. Outside of our home, she wasn't mentioned because it wasn't socially acceptable to have an adopted child of Oriental derivation. She spent most of her time playing in her room or in a secluded little garden we had prepared for her behind the house. As you may have guessed, this was her very room.

"Soon-ei had only lived with us for about a year when an incident took place that broke my heart forever and caused my husband's hair to turn white within a fortnight. Harris and I were seated in the morning room when

Theodore brought us an envelope. A stranger had left it at the door. It was a ransom note demanding five hundred thousand dollars if we were to ever see Soon-ei alive again.

"Harris ran to the backyard where she had been playing, but she was gone. Inquiries were made and all of the servants questioned, but Soon-ei was nowhere to be found. The police were summoned and a thorough investigation effected, but to no avail. The ransom money was dropped off at the time and place appointed, but we never saw our little Soon-ei again."

Sam bit his bottom lip, ashamed of his earlier words. Mrs. Holloway had certainly gone through everything he was going through now.

"My husband's family was very wealthy and owned many of the area newspapers. Everything was ordered hushed, and that was that. I'm afraid we will never know what happened to our beloved daughter. I fear that she is long dead."

Then Mrs. Holloway paused. "So you see, Sam, I do understand how you feel and what you are going through. This wretched business with dear Brenda has brought to the surface many feelings and issues that I had forced myself to forget. It has prompted me to face that which I have not been able to confront for many years."

Sam and Amberley sat in the stillness as if the slightest movement or sound would cause the setting to shatter like glass. The narrative they had just heard and the dismal room had left them solemn and sad.

Finally, Amberley stood up, pulled her chair next to Mrs. Holloway, and tenderly put her arm around her.

"Oh, Mrs. Holloway! We did not know. We could not have imagined."

Sam stood up and paused for a moment as he watched his daughter comfort Mrs. Holloway. Under the facade of an unapproachable high-society millionaire, she truly had a very tender heart.

"I'm so sorry, ma'am, that I said you did not understand. I was very wrong. Your heart is broken just like ours. Please forgive me. If you will have your lawyer draw up the papers for the loan, I will sign them," Sam said.

"Loan! Nonsense!" Mrs. Holloway said. "What good is money! One spends their whole life trying to acquire it, and what good does it do? Money is worthless unless it is used to help others. That is what Harris used to tell me, and I guess I needed to be reminded of it. It's not a loan, Sam; it's a gift. Now run along home and comfort your wife. She needs you."

* * *

The sun had not yet risen as Joe fed his livestock and gathered the morning's eggs. He felt so helpless as he thought about Brenda and wondered where she could be.

He wanted to help but didn't know how to begin. Then he remembered something his pa had told him: *If you want to find out what stinks, follow the smell!*

Joe's thoughts immediately went to Michael McGuinnes as he tried to connect the dots in his head: the vicious argument that morning in the Belmont Tavern, Mike's insulting words while Joe was painting his mailbox, the way he had parked near the Schenkle farm and watched Brenda, and his vitriolic words and humiliation at the Fireman's Picnic. McGuinnes hated Sam Bridges, but did he hate him enough to kidnap his daughter?

Joe set the basket of eggs he had gathered just inside the door of the kitchen. "Ma, I'll be back in a few."

Joe tightened the cinch of Gypsy's saddle and trotted off down Shanghai Road, stopping at a small cottage near Pipestone Creek. The lights were on in the kitchen, and Joe gave a quick knock at the door and walked right in.

"Good mornin', Aunt Peg. Is Perry up yet?" he asked.

"Yes, he should be out in a few minutes. Sit down, Joe, and have some biscuits and coffee," she said, filling his cup.

Joe split a fresh, hot, steamy biscuit and buttered it.

"Nobody can make 'em like you, Aunt Peg. I've always said that."

Aunt Peg smiled and called out, "Perry! You got company."

Perry sauntered into the kitchen with only one suspender strap on his shoulder, rubbing his eyes and finding his seat at the table.

"Joe," he nodded sleepily and took a sip of hot coffee. "What brings ya here, cuz?"

"Perry, we haven't always seen eye to eye on things, but you're my cousin and I need your help."

"'Bout what?"

"How long you worked for Mike McGuinnes? Two, three years?"

"It's been about that. Why you askin'?"

"Perry, I can't tell you that jus' now. I need to know: has McGuinnes been doin' anything odd these last few weeks?"

Perry took a bite out of his biscuit and chewed it while he thought.

"He's been gone a lot. Fact, I haven't seen him the last few days, but his girlfriend Judy's been around."

Joe sat up on the edge of his chair. "I didn't know he had a girlfriend. What does she look like?"

"'Bout thirty years old. Long blonde hair. She has this blue Buick she flies around town in an' never stops at a stop sign. Gonna kill somebody someday," Perry said, scratching his beard.

Joe thought about the empty blue Buick found wrecked in the ravine. A coincidence? Or—was someone trying to throw searchers off the scent?

"Perry, think! Does she ever drive anything else?"

Perry thought. "Well, I seen her several times gettin' groceries at the store in town, drivin' Mike's green Jeep."

"Any particular time?"

"Usually right after the store opens in the mornin'—'bout eight or nine."

"Thanks, Perry," Joe said, finishing his coffee. "Would you promise not to mention any of this to anyone, especially at work?"

"You got it!" Perry said with a wave as Joe kissed Aunt Peg and walked out the door.

Back home, Joe put Gypsy in the stall and went inside the house to talk to his mother.

"Ma, I'll be gone for several hours gettin' supplies," he said. "I'll take a sandwich and some coffee with me, so don't worry about fixin' lunch."

He threw his lunch together, started up his dad's old black Ford pickup truck, and pausing at the end of the driveway, breathed a prayer. *Dear Lord, please help me ta find Brenda. Show me where she's at.*

Joe drove down Park Road to Eau Claire and carefully slid his pickup into a parking spot at the far end of the grocery store. Contemplating a long wait, he took out his thermos to pour himself a cup of coffee, when to his surprise, McGuinnes's green Jeep pulled into the parking lot only two spaces over. He slid down in his seat and pulled the bill of his hat over his face. The blonde female driver quickly went inside the store for about half an hour and then came out with two brown bags of groceries, placing them behind the seat. Screeching her tires, she pulled out of the parking lot and sped along Main Street.

Joe started his truck and began to follow her from a distance as she turned south on Hochberger Road, leading out of town. *She must be goin' to Berrien Springs or Niles*, he thought. He was surprised, then, when the Jeep turned westward onto Hipps Hollow Road. Joe followed carefully, keeping his distance and stopping once or twice to let the vehicle get far ahead. That wasn't hard—the woman sped along like she owned the road.

Where could she be goin'? McGuinnes don't live near the hollow, Joe thought as he slammed on his brakes. The Jeep's brake lights had just flashed on as it pulled over to the opposite side of the road, directly across from the thick woods near the river. Had the woman seen him?

Joe pulled off onto an old dirt service road and watched. After about fifteen minutes, he saw two men come out of the hollow and take the bags of groceries from the woman. One of the men was Michael McGuinnes. Joe looked hard at the other man but did not recognize him. The men quickly disappeared into the woods, and the Jeep sped away.

Joe was perplexed. What had he just seen here? He had to tell someone right away, but who could he trust—and who was wise enough to figure it out?

Seventeen
The Mission

As far as Brenda could tell, she had spent the last two days in a small apartment with Michael McGuinnes and his tall blonde girlfriend. She had been tied up, but they had not hurt her. While Michael McGuinnes often sneered, Judy was always kind to her, expressing regret in private for what was happening. She seemed to be terrified of McGuinnes and sought to obey him only to avoid his ire. Then late one evening, Brenda was quickly blindfolded, put in a car, and driven to some unknown location.

"Mike, please don't hurt her. She's only a girl," Judy pleaded with McGuinnes as he unceremoniously pulled Brenda from the Jeep and began leading her along a thick, dark forest path. He had tied her hands behind her, and as he dragged her along, she lost her balance and fell.

"Pick up your feet! If you're tryin' to stall for time—forget it! No one knows where we are," McGuinnes shouted, snatching the blindfold from Brenda's face.

Brenda said nothing, but she blinked her eyes as they adjusted to the dark woods around her. Her arms began to bruise from McGuinnes's roughness, and her legs were cut and bleeding from being dragged through the vines and heavy undergrowth of the woods. It was damp and humid, and the mosquitoes bit her unmercifully.

But her captor was right. She could not imagine that anyone knew where she was. The forest was large, and not until she saw the familiar sight of the Buckles's cabin did she realize where she had been taken. Andy and Sarah Buckles were an elderly black couple who lived all alone in the woods of Hipps Hollow.

Brenda had resigned herself to what was probably going to happen. She had thought about the sequence of events since Bickel had first kidnapped her, and she could come to no other conclusion than that she was to be killed. Her father was certainly in no hurry to take her south, as he had threatened to do—she hadn't seen him since he left her at Mike McGuinnes's apartment. She knew Bickel's hatred for her and the Bridges family could not go unresolved, and from what she'd seen of McGuinnes, he was just as bitter. Even if this was somehow about money, she could not be left to identify the principles of this crime. But no matter how bad things were, she clung to her faith. If the Lord rescued her or if He did not, her destiny was completely in His hands, and she had to trust Him with it.

As they approached the cabin door, McGuinnes shouted out, "Hey! It's McGuinnes!"

The door slowly opened, squeaking on its rusty hinges. A dark figure emerged wearing a faded brown coat and a green pork pie hat.

Brenda tried to focus her eyes in the settling darkness. They were smarting from the perspiration running down from her forehead. The figure was her father.

"Good news, Bickel. It's all set up for tomorrow morning. The cash will be left at the place we agreed, all in tens and twenties."

"So the old widow came through. I thought she would," Bickel said, rubbing his hands together with glee. He sneered at Brenda and pointed to the cabin. "Well, get her inside with the others!"

Michael McGuinnes grinned in his amusement at the fear in Brenda's eyes. *If Sam Bridges could only be here . . . how beautiful!* he thought.

As she blinked away tears and settled into a corner of the cabin, Brenda saw Andy and Sarah, tied up and blindfolded. She looked at her father and Michael McGuinnes as they chatted together. She knew that sometimes a terrorist or an activist would do things like this for a strong belief or cause, but this was pure evil, motivated by greed and hate. Brenda stretched her legs in an effort to comfort herself and settled into her little nest of resignation.

* * *

Life in Old Sodus

It was mid-morning, and Mary decided to make an early lunch. No one was really hungry, and she was only cooking out of habit. Amberley and Lien were sent to school that morning to keep their lives as routine as possible. Sam sat at the table with his coffee, sure that the next phone call from Brenda's kidnappers would come today.

There was a sudden knock at the back door, and Mary opened it.

"Why, Joe! Please come in," Mary said.

"Thank you, ma'am, but may I speak to Mr. Bridges outside?"

Sam stepped out the back door, and they sat together on the tailgate of his pickup truck. "What is it, Joe?" Sam asked.

Joe looked at the ground, searching for the words to say. "Sir, I look up to ya, like a father, you know. You are powerful upset about Brenda and so am I, but I need ya to hear me out."

Joe explained his suspicions about Michael McGuinnes and what he had seen that morning as best he could. Sam was riveted by the details, and after asking a number of questions, he rushed into the house and returned with a map of Hipps Hollow.

"You say it was about here, Joe?"

"Yes, sir!"

Sam smiled for the first time in several days. Where Joe had seen the green Jeep and Michael McGuinnes was directly adjacent to Buckles Hollow and the cabin belonging to his old friends.

"Thanks, Joe. If this works out, you will be the hero of the story. I will see you later."

Sam hopped off the tailgate to return to the house when Joe grabbed him by the arm.

"Mr. Bridges, wait! You got somethin' in mind, don't you? You're gonna try and rescue Brenda."

Sam cocked his head to the side, looking at the young man thoughtfully. "Joe, go home now and don't say anything to anybody about this. Okay?"

"Mr. Bridges, ya gotta let me go with you. I can help. You can't do this alone."

"Joe, I can't take the chance of you getting hurt. What would happen to your ma?"

Joe scooted off the tailgate and stood tall. "I'm eighteen and a man, Mr. Bridges. You told me that yourself. Now I've heard tell that Green Berets are teachers. You have taught others, so teach me! I will obey you in everything ya say."

Sam looked into Joe's eyes. They were as sincere as they were determined.

"Mary," Sam said, sticking his head inside the door, "Joe and I are going for a walk."

Sam folded the map of the hollow and put it into his hip pocket as he and Joe walked to the bench in front of the post office.

"Joe, I'm going to be brutally honest with you. I may have to do some things today that very few eighteen-year-olds have ever seen. I will have to use everything I know, everything I have ever learned, to pull this one off. There is a chance I might not make it. And no matter how it turns out, I would be severely criticized for taking you along, eighteen or not. I will also be taken to task for not letting the police handle it."

"Mr. Bridges, why aren't you tellin' the police?"

"Because the police will rush in, surround the cabin and try to talk McGuinnes and his buddy into giving up. I know Mike McGuinnes. He is like a bulldog. Once he gets his jaws around your ankle, he won't let go. He and his friend, whoever he is, have obviously thought this thing through and are prepared to stick it out to the death. That means that if they have to, they will kill any hostages and themselves. When Mike and I were very young, just before I went into the army, I found out that he had been stealing and doing some other things I can't mention. I turned him in, and he spent a long time in prison. He hates me for it, and I know that somehow, he is using Brenda to make me pay. This is personal. No, I have to go another route."

"What are you gonna do, sir?" Joe asked, beginning to see the problem.

"I must change their game plan, set them off balance, and make them weak. I have to turn everything around on them."

Sam stood up and smiled at Joe. "But there is something you can do if you really want to help."

"Anything ta help Brenda, sir."

"At some point I'm going to need the police. I'll call the sheriff and tell him to be waiting for your call. I'm giving you the responsibility of calling him and bringing him to the right spot. Meet me here at dusk, and I will have the timeline worked out. Remember, Joe, nothing about this mission to anybody."

Joe smiled at the word "mission" and nodded his head. Saving Brenda was the most important thing to him now, and working with a real Green Beret made it exciting.

Eighteen
The Hunter

Sam reached over and turned off his headlights and ignition switch, letting his pickup truck coast down the hill near the spot where Joe had seen McGuinnes. Slowly and methodically, he put it in gear, careful not to tap the brake lights. He rolled down the window to listen. All was dark and still except for the buzzing of insects, the chirping of tree frogs, and the occasional croaking of a bullfrog in a distant slough.

Carefully, Sam grasped the handle of his door. But first, he reached up and removed the bulb from the dome light. Standing outside beside the truck bed, he reached into an olive-drab canvas bag to retrieve his old army web gear. This was a heavy woven utility belt and a shoulder harness. He quickly buckled it on. Finally, he slid his razor-sharp army knife into its sheath, which hung upside down from the harness strap that lay across his heart.

Sam reached into a small pouch on his belt, pulled out a tube of camouflage paint, and carefully smeared it on his face and the backs of his hands to take the shine off his skin. The feel and smell of it was familiar. It made him remember preparing for the many missions he had led and participated in while fighting in Vietnam. He had always worried about his men and whether or not they would be coming back alive. Sam was older now. Did he still have what it took to get the job done? He smiled a faint smile and then shook his head. *I have no choice,* he thought, as he patted insect repellent called "bug juice" on his clothing and the back of his neck from a small green squeeze bottle.

Satisfied, he reached into the truck bed and picked up an object wrapped in a long dark cloth. Carefully, he unwound it. There, meticulously preserved, was a wooden crossbow and a bamboo quiver of arrows called bolts. Sam had decided not to bring a firearm along. Everything about what he was going to do relied upon stealth. If he had to use deadly force, a rifle would only give him perhaps one chance, and in the dark it would reveal his position. The crossbow could be used again and again, without much sound or any muzzle flash, and he had learned to be proficient with it. Besides, in keeping with his plan, a silent arrow from the dark would be a much more frightening thing.

The crossbow had been a gift to Sam from the chief of a Montagnard tribe, a brave, loyal, hard-fighting people that lived in the central highlands of South Vietnam. They were admired and respected by the Special Forces, who did everything they could to help them. To the Vietnamese lowlanders who generally despised them, they were the Mois—dirty savages! But to Sam they were a wonderful, fearless people who were willing to die to save their Special Forces counterparts. He still remembered those who had died to save him.

As Sam waited patiently for the rods and cones in his eyes to adjust to the blackness of the night, the darkness soon became shadows, and the shadows became images. He was not at all afraid, but exhilarated. This was his element. Memories of countless all-night patrols through the steamy jungles of Southeast Asia came rushing back. Throughout his days in the war, he had been often threatened by the enemy and many times had been their hunted prey. But tonight, his precious daughter and friends were in danger, and he would bring to the surface all he had learned and experienced in those years in the Special Forces. He would do anything and everything he had to do to save them. Tonight, *he* would be the hunter!

Sam carefully cocked the crossbow and placed a single arrow along the barrel. Pressing his boonie hat on his head and slinging a length of stout rope and the bamboo quiver of arrows over his shoulder, he breathed out a pleading prayer to God for wisdom and grace.

Out of habit, Sam pulled out his army compass, but put it back in his pocket again with a slight smile. He didn't need it this time. He knew exactly where he was going and what he was going to do. He glanced at his watch. Without further hesitation, Sam melted into the darkness of the hollow as if he had somehow become a part of it.

* * *

Brenda sat on the floor of the cabin next to Sarah and Andy Buckles. Their blindfolds had been removed, and they looked at her with pitiful fear in their eyes, completely bewildered by what was happening. To Brenda's horror, McGuinnes and Bickel nonchalantly passed a bottle of whiskey back and forth, discussing the prisoners' fate as calmly as if they were planning a fishing trip.

"That was a pretty good idea, McGuinnes, pushin' that old Buick into the ravine. When they finally figure it out, we'll be gone."

McGuinnes chuckled. "I thought so too. Judy will bring the money here in the morning, and then we can split it between us. After that, I'm headed for Canada."

"I'm headed south, myself. I know places there where no one will ever find me. I live a simple life, so this money will last me until I die. What about you, McGuinnes? You and Judy live off a hundred and twenty-five grand for the rest of yer lives?"

McGuinnes chuckled. "No, but I can by myself. Judy ain't comin'!"

"What?" Bickel said surprised. "You leavin' her here?"

"You could say that. I noticed she's gotten skittish since we started this thing. I can't trust her anymore. When she brings the money to the cabin tomorrow, well, let's just say she won't be leavin' with us."

"What are you gonna do?" Bickel asked, setting down the bottle.

"When the police finally find this place, all that will be here is a burned-out cabin and what's left of four unrecognizable corpses. The two old ones, the girl, and Judy."

Bickel scratched his beard and shook his head. "I thought I had a grudge against Sam Bridges, but you got it bad for 'im. Remind me never to get on yer bad side."

Then Bickel paused, the smile fleeing from his face. "But McGuinnes," he said, pulling back his jacket to show the pistol in his belt. "Just in case you get any ideas of adding me to your list of victims and taking all the money for yourself . . ."

* * *

"Come in, Joe," Mary said with a weary smile, opening the kitchen door. "Where is Mr. Bridges?"

It was dark out now, as Joe had been outside—with Sam, Mary had assumed—for hours. Joe sat down at the kitchen table. He looked at Mary and the girls. Lien was helping Amberley, who was organizing Brenda's homework assignments. Mary had asked that Mrs. Davison continue to include Brenda in everything as if nothing had happened.

"He will be back soon. He asked me ta give you this," he said, handing her a folded sheet of paper.

The message was short, and she read it aloud.

> Mary, I've gone to get Brenda. Joe has my instructions to call the police and bring them to me at a certain time. Please do not ask him any questions now, but help him the best you can. Pray for me. Love ya . . . Sam

Mary looked up at Joe, in spite of the letter, hoping he would tell her more, but he was resolute. He had to obey Mr. Bridges.

* * *

Bickel looked at his watch. It was past nine o'clock.

"McGuinnes, we better start taking them outside for their last break."

"I'll take the old ones out first. They won't give me any problems. The girl I'll take by herself. She might get ideas to struggle and run," McGuinnes said.

McGuinnes returned to the cabin with the Buckles, who were barely able to stand. As they found their places in the corner on the floor, McGuinnes yanked Brenda to her feet by her sore and bruised arm. He untied the rope from her wrists and stuffed it in his jacket pocket.

"Here now," he said gruffly. "Don't you be trying anything!"

Brenda rubbed her sore wrists as she walked in front of McGuinnes to the old wooden outhouse in the distance. As she stumbled along on the uneven ground, a sudden notion came over her, and she drew a deep breath. *They are going to kill me anyway*, she thought. She didn't know Buckles Hollow as well as Amberley did, but she was sure that Grandma Andrews's farm was to the west of the cabin.

Breathing out a prayer to God for help, she quickly turned, pushed past McGuinnes, and broke into a run. He swiftly gained his composure and chased after her. As Brenda hurried along the dark and dense path, it seemed that every vine and thorny bush reached out to grab her. She dashed through a stand of maple saplings and felt the sting of their whiplike branches across her face. McGuinnes was not far behind, for she could hear his grunting close on her heels. She knew that if he caught her, he would probably kill her then and there.

"Come here, you little scamp! Wait till I get a hold of you!" McGuinnes shouted.

As he grabbed for her sleeve, a blur of movement caught the corner of her eye. There was the sound of a dull thud, and both he and Brenda went tumbling to the ground. As she came to rest on her side, Brenda glanced back and thought she was hallucinating, for she saw McGuinnes struggling with something or someone next to the cabin. Had Bickel had a change of heart and decided to save her as she had always hoped he would? Several more thuds—louder this time—sent McGuinnes reeling backwards and smashing against a tree.

Brenda attempted to crawl away when she felt someone grab her, and a hand quickly covered her mouth. Was it Eltie Bickel? She panicked and began to swing and resist with all her might.

"Brenda! Control yourself!" came a soft whisper into her ear.

Oh, he's got me! she thought. Then there it was, mingled with the smell of insect repellent and face paint, the familiar scent of Dad's aftershave. She stopped struggling and let her mind clear. It really *was* Dad! She hugged him tightly, too relieved to speak or cry.

"Brenda, is the man inside the cabin your father?"

"Yes," she answered.

"I thought as much. I have to lure him outside or he might use Andy and Sarah as hostages or worse. I want you to listen to me carefully, because I have no time to prepare you for what I'm going to do. You need to grow up real fast —now, this instant, and trust me and obey me with no doubting. Can you do that?"

"Yes, sir!" she whispered. "But Daddy, he's got a gun. He carries it in his belt."

"I assumed one of them did. Now, as quietly as you can, move back into the woods and stay low. If this goes badly, I want you to crawl out of here on your hands and knees to the road. The pickup is there and the keys are in it. Don't try to help me, just go! No matter what you see here, you must remain quiet and do exactly as I say. Do you understand?"

She nodded with a slight smile as her father kissed her on the cheek. With tears of relief in her eyes, she moved a safe distance into the woods.

Instantly, Sam took the long rope he had slung over his shoulder, tied it under the arms of the unconscious McGuinnes, and tossed the other end over a low hanging branch. He pulled McGuinnes to a standing position. For several moments, Sam looked into the face of Michael McGuinnes and thought about what he had done to Brenda —what he would have done if he'd had the chance. A fleeting notion crossed Sam's mind. If this had been Vietnam and the war, McGuinnes would be nothing more than the enemy, human refuse to be easily disposed of with no mercy, no regrets. But the Lord had long ago gotten hold of Sam, and he must now play by a different set of rules.

With several hard pulls, Sam yanked McGuinnes to his feet with only the tips of his toes touching the ground. A final quick snap of the rope caused the man to cry out in pain. Sam quickly tethered the other end of the rope to the tree and then faded back into the woods as McGuinnes began to struggle and shout out to his companion for help.

"Bickel! Bickel! Come help me! Bickel!"

Eltie Bickel kicked the door open in his haste, sending it flying off of its rusted hinges. As a dim shaft of light spilled out into the woods, he rushed over the threshold, waving the pistol in his hand. He stopped for a moment to allow his eyes to adjust to the darkness, aghast at the image of his partner suspended from a tree. His eyes quickly darted from side to side like a cornered beast.

"Who are you? What do you want?" he shouted out, his voice shaking, but no answer came.

In his panic, the man aimed his pistol into the darkness and pulled the trigger. The flame from the barrel shot out several feet into the blackness of the night. He began firing randomly in all directions, hoping to strike his invisible enemy. Brenda hunkered down as flat as she could, hearing the stray bullets zing through the trees.

"Bickel, you crazy fool! You're going to hit me!" McGuinnes shouted.

Then suddenly there was a muffled snap, and all was silent. The pistol dropped from Bickel's hand, and with an expression of horror, he looked down to see a single arrow deeply embedded in his right shoulder.

Bewildered and in a final effort to save himself, he dashed off into the darkness. Another dull thud came from the trees, and soon, Sam Bridges reappeared from the dark with his crossbow in his hand, carrying the unconscious Bickel over his shoulder. Dropping him hard on the ground, Sam quickly tied him to the tree next to his partner and shouted out for Brenda, who could scarcely believe what she had just witnessed.

She ran to her father but stopped abruptly in front of the two men.

"Dad? Are they . . . ?" She hesitated.

"They'll live. Let's go see to the Buckles."

Sam hurried through the cabin door, contemplating any horror he might find. He sighed with relief at the sight that met his eyes: seated opposite the doorway were Andy and Sarah, tied up on the floor—and very much alive. Sam pulled his knife from its sheath and quickly cut the ropes that held them as Brenda helped them to their feet and into chairs. Without orders, she started going through the cupboards, pulling out coffee and a pot to make it in. Her hands were shaking, but she needed to help Dad and the Buckles now.

Andy and Sarah were stunned and frightened, and not until Brenda gave them hot coffee were they able to speak.

"We wuz so scared, Sam! They came in several days ago an' tied us up. They was gonna kill us and burn the cabin," Andy gasped.

Brenda put her arms around Sarah and held her tenderly. She was shivering and couldn't speak.

"It's all over, Andy. They can't hurt you anymore," Sam said, rubbing Andy's shoulder.

Brenda looked up at her adopted father, the only real father she'd ever had, standing in the dim lamplight. His face and hands were streaked with shades of green and black camouflage paint, and he was wearing the faded tiger fatigues he had worn in Vietnam. On his arm was an arrow-shaped patch with a sword and three lightning bolts. She had seen it many times before, but this was the first time she truly understood what it meant. Her father would always be a Green Beret. It was forever a part of who he was.

Amberley had told her about the times before Sam had become a Christian. He had been an alcoholic and lived a discouraged, defeated life. She had wondered how Ma could have put up with it all, but now she was able to see what Ma had seen all along. All at once, Sam was more truly her brave knight and hero than he had ever been.

How wonderful, she thought with glistening eyes, *that the bravest, sweetest, kindest man in the whole world just happens to be my dad!*

Nineteen
Reversing the Fear

Joe led Sheriff Warner to Buckles Hollow at the appointed time, and he took the men into custody.

"I've known Michael McGuinnes for most of my life, and this is about the way I figured it would end for him. I was the one who arrested him and sent him off to prison, back when I was a young deputy. Evidently, he knew of Andy and Sarah's cabin and found it an attractive hideout. I'm sure the Buckles owe you their very lives, Sam. If the two men had left the area, I doubt if we would have ever caught them," Sheriff Warner said soberly.

"What I did was relatively easy, Sheriff. Joe here did the detective work and put two and two together. I didn't want to hurt Bickel, but he began firing his pistol all over the woods. I was afraid he might hit Brenda."

Sheriff Warner smiled. "Don't give it another thought, Sam. What this guy got was a bee sting compared to what he deserved. Considering what these men had planned for your daughter and the Buckles, they got away mighty easy. You could have made them both into pincushions." He patted Sam on the shoulder. "I'm sure McGuinnes's girlfriend will sing like a bird when she finds out that he intended to do her in too!"

Then he paused. "Sam?" he asked seriously. "Why didn't you come to me first? Me and my deputies could have helped you."

"No disrespect, Sheriff, but this wasn't a routine police matter. It required a special touch. I had to get those guys out of that cabin and rescue my daughter and the Buckles at the same time. Their strength was in the fear and terror they were imposing on others. It put them in control and gave them confidence. I had to reverse the fear and make them weak. If they knew the police were outside, they certainly would have kept their captives as hostages. They would not have been afraid to kill anyone, including themselves."

Sam smiled. "I hope you're not vexed with me, Sheriff."

Sheriff Warner paused and then grinned. "No, Sam, if I had your training and experience, and that was my daughter in there, I would have done the same. Likely I would have done worse. You're a man of integrity."

Later, after Doctor Cumberland had attended to Brenda's cuts and bruises, she sat down next to Ma on the couch in Grandma's living room. Grandma Andrews was waiting at the kitchen table while the doctor examined the Buckles.

"Sweetie, are you going to be all right?" Mary asked gently. "Do you want to speak to Pastor Mitchell?"

"No, Ma," she said thoughtfully, leaning her head against Ma's shoulder. "I think I have it all under control. I lived a pretty rough life before I was saved and I met you. I guess my feathers don't ruffle that easily anymore. Besides, the Lord has given me the peace and understanding that I need."

She paused. "Ma? I am so proud of Dad. He is so brave and wonderful. I hope I meet someone like him someday."

"I think you may have, sweetie. You just don't know it yet," Ma said, kissing Brenda on the forehead.

Dr. Cumberland came out of the spare bedroom just off of the kitchen, and as he softly closed the door behind him, he peeked around the corner into the living room.

"Mary?" he said. "May I speak with you and Marian in the kitchen?" Ma nodded and left Brenda curled up on the couch, following Dr. Cumberland into the kitchen.

"I think Andy and Sarah will be all right," the doctor said, setting his satchel down on the corner of the kitchen table. "I've given them something to help them rest. Now, you know they can't go back to that shack in the woods after this. They were getting too old and feeble to live there much longer anyway, and this has been a shock. What are your plans?"

"I don't know, Doctor," Grandma Andrews said, "but they can stay with me as long as they want. I don't know if they have anyone else in this old world but themselves."

"Well, fortunately for them they have you folks as friends. I'll stop by tomorrow to check on them and Brenda."

Amberley quietly entered the living room and sat in a chair opposite Brenda, who had closed her eyes to rest. After a few moments, she opened her eyes to see her sister staring at her pitifully.

Brenda smiled and patted the cushion next to her. "Come and sit next to me, sis."

Amberley shyly sat down and then began to cry. "Oh, Brenda, I'm so sorry. How terrible this has been. I'm so ashamed of myself."

Brenda reached out and hugged her sister. "I wouldn't let you explain. I should have known that you wouldn't do anything to hurt me. You were just looking out for me the best you could."

"Brenda, I . . . I do love you. I was afraid that I wouldn't get a chance to say those words to you again. I am sorry that I got so angry with you."

Brenda smiled. "You sure let me know what for. I didn't think you had it in you, but I had it coming. Let's try never to have a falling-out again."

"Never," Amberley whispered.

Sam took the girls back home to the village, but Mary stayed with Grandma Andrews to help look after the Buckles. After several days, Andy was recovering fine, but Sarah seemed to be still in shock. She would not leave her room, and she spoke to no one. Andy and Mary tried to coax her into eating, but she would only drink some juice. The terrible ordeal had been too much for her. She would constantly stare at the door as if she expected the kidnappers to suddenly reappear.

"Sarah is still not gettin' along, Mary," Andy said sadly. "Do ya think Pastor Mitchell would talk ta her?"

"I'm sure he would, Andy. I'll see if he can come over this afternoon."

The Buckles were Christians and had long attended church on the Sodus side of Townline Road. They now rarely got out of the hollow at all, so Pastor Mitchell would visit them every week and have devotions with them. Andy was visibly relieved when the pastor arrived at the house.

Pastor Mitchell spoke with Sarah, and she seemed to respond to his wise counsel and kindness. Gently but firmly, Pastor said, "Sarah, I know that what you went through was terrible, and I don't want to make it seem like it wasn't. You and Andy had a very close call, but the Lord knew all along that this was going to happen, and with it provided an escape.

"You know, unsaved folks can sit around in fear and hopelessness, but we can't. The Lord commanded us not to live in fear and not to be anxious about what tomorrow may bring. Those men were powerless to do anything to you unless they were first permitted by God Himself."

Sarah smiled as Pastor reached out and held her hand.

"Do you think for one moment that the Lord did not know that you were in trouble? God knew and sent Sam Bridges to deliver you." Pastor smiled and patted her hand.

Sarah smiled too and began to softly weep.

"You're right, Preacher. I know everythin' you say is true. I guess I just needed to be reminded," Sarah said. "Shame on me for not trustin' the Lord when everything was always in His hands!"

Pastor Mitchell prayed with Sarah and then came out into the kitchen.

"Please have some coffee, Pastor," Mary said.

"Thanks, Mary. Sarah should be all right now. She is just like most of us. We don't need to be taught new truth as much as we need to be reminded of the old! She had just forgotten that there are no surprises in the life of a child of God."

Andy left the kitchen to be with Sarah.

Pastor spoke softly to Mary. "What are you going to do about the Buckles, Mary?"

"I don't know, Pastor. My mother said they can stay with her. Sam heard something about a daughter who lives out in Ohio or Indiana, but no one can confirm it. Andy claims he has no blood kin living anywhere, so we are at a dead end. When asked about a daughter, he changes the subject. It's obvious they can't go back to live in the hollow anymore. The memories of what happened are there, and their secure little world no longer exists for them."

Pastor set down his cup and stood up.

"What you say about a daughter is intriguing. I know some people who have known the Buckles for many years. Let me make some inquiries and get back with you. Thanks for the coffee, Mary," Pastor said.

"Sarah should be all right tonight. Thank you, Pastor, for coming out. We appreciate you so much."

Days passed with no word from Pastor Mitchell, and the Buckles settled in with Grandma Andrews. Sam went over to Buckles Hollow every morning to feed the cow and the chickens. He thought about looking around the small cabin for some evidence of a distant relative—but if there was someone, the Buckles were keeping it a secret, and he didn't want to intrude.

Twenty
Mending Fences

Several days had passed, and on Friday morning the girls made ready for school. Mary wanted Brenda to stay home for the whole week and rest, but she begged her to let her go.

"I want to get back to normal as soon as I can, Ma. I feel fine. Really I do," Brenda pleaded.

"Okay, sweetie," Mary said with some apprehension. "Only please take care. You have been through a lot."

"I will, Ma."

It was the beginning of a beautiful, warm day, and the orchards in Sodus Township were heavy with ripening apples. Brenda was quiet and deep in thought as she peddled to school beside Amberley. Despite her insistence that she was fine, the events of a week ago were beginning to sink in. As she thought about the things she'd heard Eltie Bickel say—his total lack of regard for her, his selfishness—they made her sad. She had always hoped that he would change. He had been her father, and though he was a rascal and a scoundrel, she could not help having feelings for him.

Whether or not she would be able to do anything as noble as visit or write him in the future, she couldn't tell. For now, that would have to be left to the passing of time.

* * *

The girls left River School on their bikes that afternoon and peddled the dusty two miles home. As they turned down the alley beside their house, they saw a shiny red car blocking the way. Brenda pulled up beside it and noticed an envelope tied to the radio antenna with a ribbon. It was simply addressed to "Amberley and Brenda Bridges."

Brenda handed the envelope to her sister. Amberley slowly opened it and pulled out the car's title and a letter. She read it aloud:

> Dear Ladies,
> Congratulations on getting your driver's licenses. Please accept this automobile as a gift from me. We had a bargain, and I failed to live up to my end. The car has been completely restored and should be trouble free.
> Sincerely,
> K. H. Holloway

"The Studebaker!" Amberley shouted. "She gave us the Studebaker!"

"It's beautiful!" Brenda declared. "Look at all the work she got done!"

"Wait a minute, girls!" came a voice from behind them.

Amberley and Brenda turned to look. There stood Dad by the steps with his arms folded.

"I don't want to throw a wet blanket on your party, but haven't you forgotten something? What about *our* deal? How are you going to afford the insurance and upkeep on this vehicle?" Dad smiled tenderly. "Besides, you really didn't earn it, did you?"

Amberley and Brenda looked at each other with their mouths open. They had forgotten all about their part of the responsibility. What were they going to do? They had no money for a car.

"I guess we're going to have to give the car back," Amberley said sadly.

Sam's face was soft, but his voice was still serious. "I'm sorry, girls. I really am, but there is no way your mother and I can afford to pay for two vehicles. We are trying desperately to save for your college tuition. You will have to take it back."

After supper, Amberley carefully drove the bright red Studebaker down Naomi Road to King's Landing. Brenda sat in the passenger seat, trying to savor the first and last ride in the beautiful car.

"Do you think we set some kind of record for the shortest period of time for owning a car?" Brenda asked.

"Perhaps," Amberley said, "but we really didn't own it, and besides, we certainly didn't earn it. Dad is right in making us take it back. Mrs. Holloway is kind of strange anyway. Maybe next week she might change her mind and ask for it back."

"Well, here we are," Brenda lamented as they pulled up to the gates of the estate. "I wish we could just leave it and run. I don't look forward to facing Theodore again."

"Neither do I," Amberley agreed. "He acts as if he is disgusted to see us."

Amberley parked the car under the large overhang at the front door. The girls quickly walked up the steps, and without hesitation, Brenda banged the knocker hard and stepped back to wait.

After a moment, the huge oak door swung open, and there stood Theodore. Looking from Amberley to Brenda and back again, he uttered his usual woodnotes of "Dear me!" and disappeared into the house.

Brenda looked over at Amberley in silence, raising one eyebrow to show her growing impatience with the unfriendly butler. After an eternity of five minutes, Theodore reappeared at the door and led them into the beautiful morning room.

"I was hoping you would come to see me," said Mrs. Holloway kindly, seated in her personal jungle.

"Thank you, ma'am," the girls said in unison, taking a seat. After a moment of silence, they looked at each other in hopes that the other would speak first.

"Mrs. Holloway?" Brenda finally spoke. "We want to thank you for the beautiful car, but we can't keep it. It is not right that we take something we haven't properly earned. Besides, we can't really afford a car right now."

"The car is a small gift from me to you. Please don't hurt my feelings by giving it back," said Mrs. Holloway.

Amberley cleared her throat. "We had an agreement with our father that when we got our first car, we would have jobs to help pay for insurance and gasoline. We are trying to find after-school jobs now to help save for college. We won't be able to afford both."

"We appreciate your kindness, ma'am, but we must obey our father. We know he is right," Brenda said.

As skillfully as a defense attorney, Mrs. Holloway made her case for allowing the girls to keep the car as a gift.

"You may think me strange, ladies, but I have much for which to atone. I want to help you and your sister Lien as much as I can. I know that your father will not allow you to receive charity, but I will speak with him. Perhaps because of our long association and recent events, he will listen to me and will allow you to earn your automobile, and perhaps I can help you with the expenses. It is, after all, my fault you didn't earn it. I offered you employment and then reneged on the bargain. Your father is a good, honest man, and in some respects, reminds me of my own Harris. That is why, perhaps, I have always liked him and wanted to help him."

"Mrs. Holloway, would you like to come for Sunday dinner tomorrow?" Amberley blurted out. "I know that our folks would like to have you."

Mrs. Holloway was surprised. "I . . . I would like that very much, if you think they won't mind. I am most anxious to meet your little sister Lien."

"We will expect you at one o'clock. We attend church in the morning but would enjoy your company for dinner," Amberley said, standing.

Brenda reached over and took Mrs. Holloway's hand. "And thank you, ma'am, for all that you did to help me. Dad and Amberley told me about the money and—and your daughter. Please don't grieve so. You can't change the past, but you can live for the future. I worry about you sitting alone in this old house," she said with great sincerity.

Mrs. Holloway smiled and dried her eyes with her handkerchief.

"Do you, dear? That's the sweetest thing anyone has said to me in years," she said and leaned over to kiss Brenda on the cheek.

* * *

As the girls walked slowly home, they discussed what they were going to tell their parents.

"That was very mature of you, Amber, inviting Mrs. Holloway to dinner. I was impressed," Brenda said.

Amberley smiled. "Perhaps I should have asked Ma first."

"I think it will be all right. What you did was so like Ma," Brenda said. "I guess you are finally growing up."

When the girls arrived back home, they told their mother about the dinner invitation.

"I think I will call Mrs. Holloway right away and tell her that she is very welcome for dinner tomorrow. That was very good of you to ask her, Amber," Mary said.

Sunday dinner was thoroughly enjoyable. Ma had made a large pork roast from one of Grandma Andrews's fat hogs, with brown, crisp skin and luscious, juicy meat that fell apart when forked. Brenda made the mashed potatoes, whipped with roasted garlic and fresh creamery butter from the House of David Dairy. Amberley made a pan of fresh-baked golden-brown biscuits oozing with white cheddar cheese and herbs. Lien helped Ma make the vegetable: creamed yellow wax beans and pearl onions from Joe's summer garden. Dessert was apple crumble, made by Mrs. Holloway's housekeeper, Thelmy.

Mrs. Holloway proved to be quite the conversationalist—and very convincing when she wanted to be. At her behest, Sam and Mary agreed to allow the girls to work for a few hours each Saturday to work off the Studebaker. In addition, she would also pay them a little something to help cover gasoline and insurance.

Mrs. Holloway seemed stunned when she first met Lien. She begged everyone's pardon several times for her tears as she gave her a long hug. Then she opened her purse and pulled out a small photograph of Soon-ei.

"This is the only one I have. I always thought there would be time to take more," she said as she handed the photograph to Mary.

Mary was shocked! The photograph of Soon-ei was almost the exact image of Lien. No wonder Mrs. Holloway had reacted with such emotion at dinner that day. It was clear that seeing Lien had brought much of the buried past to the surface.

"You can see why this is such an emotional thing for me. I have spent many years in torment, not knowing if my little girl is alive or dead."

Mary, with her keen sense of propriety, quickly spoke up.

"Girls! It's time for coffee and Thelmy's apple crumble! Sam, would you please step down the alley to the Enkins's and get the carton of ice cream I am keeping in their freezer?"

As the girls all flocked to the kitchen and Sam left the room, Mary scooted over next to Mrs. Holloway and put her arm around her shoulder.

"Mrs. Holloway, Sam and I want to thank you with all our hearts for being willing to help us with the ransom money," Mary said softly. "We didn't know what else to do. I also want to thank you for the interest you have taken in our daughters. You are most kind. I want you to know that you are always welcome here. Please feel free to call me anytime you want to talk."

Mrs. Holloway sniffled. "Please call me Katie. I am so weary of being treated differently because I am a Holloway. I miss having friends who call me by my first name. When I first heard about poor Brenda, it went through my heart like a sword. I was glad to help because I felt as if, in some strange way, I was helping my own daughter too."

"Katie, please call me Mary. And perhaps you would like to come to church with us sometime. I think you would enjoy it."

Mrs. Holloway's face lit up. "I have wanted to visit your church in Sodus for years, but no one ever asked me. Would tonight be too soon?"

"Tonight would be just right, Katie. Let's sample the wonderful dessert you brought with some coffee, and then afterward we can talk. Sam should be back with the ice cream any minute now."

Twenty-One
Andy and Sarah's Mystery

The October wind blew blustery and cool as a waxing crescent moon hung above the town coal yard like an ornament. Sam and Mary shook hands with Pastor Mitchell at the close of the midweek service, and he asked them to remain behind to meet with him. He seemed very excited as he opened the door of his study and quickly showed them to the comfortable couch against the wall.

"I have been so keyed up by the news that I didn't think I could contain myself until the meeting tonight," said Pastor Mitchell with a bright smile. "I have been making inquires here and there and following a lot of leads. I have made dozens of phone calls, and yes!—Andy and Sarah Buckles have a foster daughter living in Indianapolis."

Sam and Mary were surprised, sitting up straight and looking at each other.

"This is unexpected news indeed. Who is she?" Mary asked.

"The information that I have is that she is—get this—a medical doctor, and a widow with several children. Did you ever imagine that two dirt-poor people like the Buckles could have a daughter who is a doctor?"

"I guess the obvious question is what happened?" Sam asked.

Rubbing his hands, Pastor Mitchell began the strange account of the early life of Andy and Sarah Buckles.

"All I've been able to ascertain is that Andy and Sarah raised this little orphan girl, and when the time came, they sold off the last few acres of their prime land to send her to school in the east. She was enrolled in a boarding school and evidently did very well. She earned several scholarships and was able to go to medical school."

"But how could she just abandon her foster parents? How could she be so ungrateful?" Mary burst out.

"Well, don't be too hasty to judge the situation. I actually spoke with their daughter earlier today on the phone." Pastor rose from his chair and sat on the edge of his desk. "She was shocked to hear that the Buckles were even alive. Apparently, for some reason known only to them, Andy and Sarah wished her to think they were dead. Word came to her shortly after she enrolled in school that they had been killed. She was told their last desire was for her to stay in school and make them proud. She was told to make a new life for herself and that there was no reason for her to ever return to Michigan."

"How odd! Andy and Sarah are hiding something—but what? And why?" Mary said.

"Well, perhaps we will soon get to the bottom of this mystery, because she is coming here on Saturday. I am picking her up at Ross Field in Benton Harbor at ten o'clock. Her name is Doctor Sonny Grayson, and she will be bringing her twin son and daughter. Can you guess their names?"

"Logically speaking, I would say Andrew and Sarah," Sam said.

Pastor Mitchell grinned. "You're right, Sam. She named her twins after her foster parents, so the problem isn't on her part. I guess we'll have to wait until she gets here to sort it out."

"But what about Andy and Sarah? Shouldn't we tell them she is coming?" Mary asked.

"That's a hard one to call, Mary," Pastor said. "I'm almost inclined to leave matters alone until she gets here. If there is a problem with their daughter, news of her visit will only cause undue anxiety. But this must be resolved, not only for them, but for their daughter's sake."

Sam nodded. "Pastor's right, Mary. Let's stay out of it unless they ask us."

* * *

Saturday morning was sunny and blue, and the three sisters were up early making breakfast. Mrs. Holloway would be picking them up to go shopping, and they were all excited.

"Mrs. Holloway is going to let us drive her Bentley, Ma," Brenda said.

"Please be careful, girls; those British cars can't decide which side of the road to drive on," Ma said with a smile.

"We will, Ma," Amberley said.

Amberley slid a long tray of biscuits into the hot oven and hurried upstairs with her sisters to get ready.

Sam had gone to pick up the Buckles from the farm. Mary had invited them over for dinner and to spend the day as a pretense. When they arrived, she felt guilty and nervous that she had deceived her two old friends—but it was necessary and for their own good.

"Sit down, folks, and have some coffee," she said when they arrived. As Mary poured Andy's coffee, she accidentally bumped his cup, spilling it on the table.

"Oh, I'm so sorry!" she said. "I'll get a towel."

"I'll get it," Sarah said, retrieving the towel from the edge of the sink.

"Thank you, Sarah," Mary said, as she repeatedly glanced out the window into the alley.

"Mary?" Andy said. "Ain't them biscuits 'bout done? I smell somethin' gettin' awful hot."

"Oh, my!" Mary said, grabbing a potholder and pulling the overly brown tray of biscuits from the oven.

"Mary, slow down," Sarah said smiling. "It's just us, child."

Sam stood up from the other end of the table to give his wife a hand.

"Mary," he said, leaning forward and whispering in her ear, "you're starting to make everyone a little crazy. Calm down. It will be all right."

Mary reached over to turn off the oven and looked into Sam's face. He smiled and winked at her.

"Sorry, everyone," she said, sitting down at the table. "This has been just one of those mornings for me."

It was ten o'clock sharp when Mrs. Holloway pulled up in front of the house.

"Mrs. Holloway is here!" Lien announced as she breezed through the kitchen to open the door.

Mrs. Holloway walked over the threshold and stood smiling.

"Hello, all! A beautiful morning, is it not?" she said cheerfully. Mrs. Holloway wore a navy blue skirt and sweater, and out of habit, carried her umbrella in the crook of her arm. Still dressed conservatively, she was a bit more stylish than the old-fashioned lace she had worn the first time the girls had met her.

"Good morning, my dear," she said, touching Lien on the cheek. "You are so radiant!"

Lien blushed. "Thank you, ma'am. Amber and Brenda will be down in a moment."

Mary welcomed her to sit down at the table for a cup of coffee. "Katie," she said, "this is Andy and Sarah Buckles, our good friends from the hollow." Mary had thought Mrs. Holloway might be surprised to see a black couple in their home, but if she was, she didn't show it.

Mrs. Holloway adjusted herself in her chair, and holding her umbrella across her arm like a scepter, she looked hard at the Buckles.

"Andy and Sarah, is it? May I call you that?" she said, leaning a little forward to peer at them. "I am Mrs. Holloway. I heard of your terrible experience in the hollow. Are you well?"

"Thank'ee kindly, ma'am," Andy said. "We are well and as good as ta be expected."

"You must be the kind lady from King's Landing our girls have told us about," Sarah said.

Just then, Amberley and Brenda came down the stairs, first hugging and kissing the Buckles and then planting a tender kiss each on Mrs. Holloway's cheek. Surprised, she reached up and touched the spot. She looked about the room into each and every face and thought about how everyone had accepted her. How Amberley had sought to comfort her the night of the ransom note, Brenda's expressed concern for her loneliness, and Mary's kindness at their first Sunday supper together. Her eyes moistened as she contemplated the sincerity and genuineness of this family's home, a sincerity she had not experienced hitherto in her life. The Buckles had somehow accepted her too just because she had been kind to "their girls."

She looked again at the Buckles, who were still smiling at her. Mrs. Holloway paused and then set her umbrella down, leaning it against the table leg. "Let's do this again," she said, reaching across the table to shake hands with Andy and Sarah. "Please call me Katie," she said with a softened smile and renewed sincerity. "I am so very pleased that you are well. If there is anything I can do to help you, please let me know. I mean that."

The sisters put on their jackets and made ready to leave with Mrs. Holloway when a knock came at the door. Sam glanced over at Mary with the raise of an eyebrow. Mary anxiously wiped her hands on a towel and opened the door. It was Pastor Mitchell. He stepped in and greeted everyone cordially. Then he looked at the Buckles and spoke.

"Andy and Sarah, I have someone with me I would like you to meet."

Pastor stepped aside, and there, standing with two young children, was an elegantly beautiful lady with Asian features. "This is Doctor Grayson and her children from Indianapolis. Perhaps you might know her better by the name you once called her—Sonny."

The Bridges family braced themselves for Andy and Sarah's reaction when Mrs. Holloway let out a soft moan and collapsed in her chair. Doctor Grayson quickly took off her coat and rushed to her side. As she checked her vital signs, Doctor Grayson's face registered shock as she looked at Mrs. Holloway. Quickly regaining her composure, the doctor looked up at Sam.

"She will be all right. She has just fainted. Let's take her somewhere to lie down."

Sam carried Mrs. Holloway into the living room and laid her on the couch while Mary put a damp cloth on her forehead.

Mary looked back at Andy and Sarah, who appeared to be shaken. Andy, with wide eyes, reached out and gripped Sarah's hand. Sarah was swelling with emotion, and she struggled to brush back the tears that began to fall from her eyes.

"Why do you suppose Mrs. Holloway fainted, Ma?" Amberley whispered.

"I know why," said Doctor Grayson. "It's because I am her daughter! *And* theirs," she said, nodding at the Buckles.

A hush fell over the room. Instead of Andy and Sarah's mystery being solved, the situation was more confusing than ever. Doctor Grayson seemed to be the only one who knew the answers.

Doctor Grayson held Mrs. Holloway's hand and turned to look at the Buckles, who had not yet recovered from the initial shock of seeing their foster daughter—or the subsequent shock of her announcement.

"Yes, Mrs. Holloway is my adopted mother, and I am just as shocked as you are. I haven't seen her since I was a little girl."

"But I don't understand!" Mary said. "You are the Buckleses' daughter, aren't you?"

Mrs. Holloway opened her eyes and stared at Sonny for several moments and then reached up and touched her cheek.

"Can it really be you, my little Soon-ei, after all of these years?"

Sonny felt the tears well up in her eyes and stream down her cheeks as she scrutinized her mother's face. She remembered faintly the first time she had looked into the face of Katherine Holloway that day at the airport. Captain Harris, the dear, kind soldier who had taken her from the poverty and squalor of the orphanage in Korea, had promised her a new mother. Surely, she would be as kind and loving as he—but Sonny vividly remembered the ugly silence and anger and Mrs. Holloway's clenched fist that day in the limousine. Then, as the weeks and months went by, that hard face would sometimes smile, and then one day —kindness and love were there!

"Yes, it's me, Soon-ei. Hi, Mom," she said. "I didn't think I would ever see you again."

"How is this possible? I don't understand!" Mrs. Holloway said.

"I guess we have a lot of things to talk about," Sonny said, wiping the tears from her cheeks.

Then Sonny stood up and looked hard at Andy and Sarah. "And you—I cried myself to sleep for weeks wondering what had happened to you! They told me at the boarding school that if I left to return to Michigan, there would be no one there to take me in. How could you be so cruel?"

Sarah and Andy arose from their seats, awkwardly walked over to Sonny, and put their arms around her.

"Honey, don't be too hard on us till ya hear us out. We did what we could an' thought was best for you at the time. If there'd been a way for us ta keep you here in Sodus and give you everythin' you needed, we'd a done it," Sarah said.

"But why did you let me think you were dead?"

Then Andy spoke. "Chile, when you came to us, we was told you'd been stolen into this country. Old Pastor Williams of Townline Church gave you to us, and with the help of our people, we kept ya secret in the hollow and raised ya till we could figure out how ta do good by you. It was Sarah here that got th' idea uh sellin' off some land to send you to school in the east. We knew that life would be hard for you as a Korean baby and harder yet with colored folks as parents. That's why we sent word that we was dead and made th' school keep you there. We did it 'cause we loved you."

Sarah spoke. "We could never get ya ta tell us 'bout your past, so we never knew where you really came from. We had to go on the story we wuz told by Pastor Williams."

"Yes, chile," Andy explained. "We wuz told that you had been brought over by uh colored soldier from South Bend. His wife didn't want a yellow baby so he dropped you off at Townline Church. We had no reason to believe anythin' else. Pastor Williams only wanted what was best for you, too. And there was no news in the papers 'bout no missin' child."

Mary looked at Doctor Grayson's two children, who stood against the wall, wide-eyed and visibly uncomfortable, hearing things about their mother that they did not understand.

"Girls, maybe Andy and Sarah would like to walk with you to the IGA and get an ice cream bar," Mary said, handing Brenda a five-dollar bill from a jar on the counter. "If that is all right with Doctor Grayson?"

Andy and Sarah Buckles looked at Mary, confused at hearing their names.

Sonny smiled. "I named my twins after you folks," she explained, and then turning to Mary she said, "Yes, that would be fine."

Andy and Sarah Buckles began to weep as Sonny held them tight.

"C'mon kids," Brenda said, putting her arms around the twins as the three sisters ushered them out the door.

"Well, I can see that you folks have much to talk about," Pastor Mitchell said, following the girls out the door with a smile. "If you need me, just call." And with a quick wave, he closed the door behind him.

"Folks, how about if I make us some dinner. It's getting late and you must be hungry," Mary said. "Doctor Grayson, perhaps you would like to freshen up."

"Everyone, please call me Sonny. Doctor Grayson lives in Indianapolis," Sonny said with a grin. "But I would like to get settled in a motel."

"There is a nice one not too far away," Mary said, "but Sonny, how would you like to stay at the big farm with my mother? She has plenty of room, and Andy and Sarah are living there."

"I would like that if it would not be putting her out. Thank you."

"Sarah, would you mind helping me with the dinner? You can help me peel some potatoes," Mary said, handing Sarah an apron.

Andy sat down next to Sam at the kitchen table, and Sonny returned to the couch next to Mrs. Holloway, rechecking her pulse. Mrs. Holloway had considered asking Sonny to stay with her in King's Landing, but she realized her long-missing daughter might not be comfortable there.

Katherine Holloway looked into her daughter's eyes. *I have another chance!* she thought. *God has given me another chance!*

* * *

Two days later, Sonny drove her rental car down River Road to the Holloway house. She was to return to Indiana later that morning and had been invited to breakfast by her adopted mother. Sonny was filled with misgivings. How would she react to the place where she had lived so many years ago, to the little garden and the solitary room where she had spent her year with the Holloways? Sonny had only been seven years old, and her memories were fragmented and faded.

As she pulled up under the large overhang in the front, Mrs. Holloway was already waiting for her on the top step. Theodore, the butler, seemed to be all out of sorts because his usual sequence of events had been violated by "madame." He paced behind her, wishing she would return to the house so he could announce her guest.

"Theodore? You're fidgeting like a schoolboy with a new set of clothes! Now please go inside and see to our breakfast!" Mrs. Holloway scolded.

After breakfast, Mrs. Holloway took Sonny through the house. Except for her gloomy bedroom and the old backyard playground, she remembered little of it. She would be happy to leave it. Except for her mother, it was now a part of her life that was long past and to be forgotten.

As they settled into the morning room, Theodore brought tea.

"Mom, before I go, I want to talk about what happened. I want you to know what I went through and why I didn't try to contact you all these years."

Sonny took a sip of hot tea and set her cup down.

"The night that I was taken from the little garden, the kidnappers put a hood over my head and taped my mouth shut. I don't know where they took me, but it was several hours away. I knew the kidnappers were trying to arrange a ransom payment for me because I heard them discuss it. I was kept locked up in a dirty little room for what seemed to be an eternity. When the day came for the ransom to be paid, I was sure that I would soon be going home.

"The kidnappers picked up the money and divided it among themselves. When the man who was supposed to return me received his share of the ransom, he told the others that they could do what they liked with me because he was leaving. The others in the gang were afraid to take me back for fear of getting caught. I didn't know where I was or how to get back home. I didn't even know where home was. One man even talked about killing me.

"Then one night, I was put on a train, and after a few hours and a cab ride, I was dumped off at a church with a note. I didn't know where I was. The old pastor and his wife felt sorry for me and gave me to the Buckles to raise incognito. Apparently, my kidnapping had been kept so secret that no one knew who I was. Andy and Sarah innocently thought I was all alone and did their best by me. I was too scared to tell them or anybody about my past because for a long time I didn't trust anybody."

Katherine Holloway set her cup down and looked at her daughter. "But Sonny, why didn't you try to contact us when you were older and able?"

"The night I was dropped off at the church, I was told that you and Dad had been killed during the kidnapping. The man who let me out threatened me and explained in gory detail what had been done to you. I was bewildered and in shock. I know now that it was just for effect, to keep me under control, but at the time, my whole little world crashed around me. I was warned that if I ever spoke a word of the kidnapping or tried to return home, I would be hunted down and killed. Later in my life, with the news that Andy and Sarah had died, I decided to forget about Michigan and its memories of death forever."

Mrs. Holloway said nothing as she sat next to her daughter amidst the gurgling sounds of water and the chirping of the birds high above. The ploy of her husband's family to keep the kidnapping quiet and out of the newspapers had backfired. Perhaps someone of the Buckleses' acquaintance would have told them about Soon-ei if it had been in the news. *It should have been shouted from the housetops!* she thought.

"And now, my dear, what will you do?" Mrs. Holloway asked.

"I must return to Indianapolis right away. This whole thing has caught me unprepared, and I must get back. I have an eleven-thirty flight out."

"Don't you want to move back here, dear? This is your home," Mrs. Holloway said.

"No, Mom. My life is in Indianapolis now, and always will be. I have a medical practice and my hands full with raising three children."

"Three? I thought you just had Andy and Sarah!" Mrs. Holloway said, surprised.

Sonny smiled. "I named my twins Andrew and Sarah after the Buckles. I have a two-year-old girl back home too. I named her Katherine after you, Mom. I was saving that as a surprise." She drew a small package wrapped in colorful paper and ribbon from her purse. "And here, Mom. I have something else for you," she said.

Mrs. Holloway took the gift, and after a moment of hesitation, she opened it. It was a family portrait of Sonny and her three children.

"I wanted you to have something to remember us by."

Then Sonny grew serious.

"Mom, I am going to take the Buckles back to Indianapolis with me. I owe them so much, and I want them to live out their final days in comfort."

Mrs. Holloway said nothing as she and Sonny stood up and began to walk the long corridor to the front door. Conflicting emotions scattered across her face, but she said nothing. Sonny saw her mother's strange expression and understood it.

"But Mom, don't you see? I want you to come along too! Won't you sell this old place and come live with me? You can bring Theodore and Thelmy along. I have a big house with plenty of room. I want the most important people in my life around me. I've lived so long without anyone—without any of you. Please say you will."

Mrs. Holloway put a hand to her mouth, and closing her eyes, she turned away. "My life is here. My roots are here. This is my home, and I cannot forsake it. I understand that you must go back to your work, and I am happy that you are caring for the Buckles, but . . ." Mrs. Holloway turned again to face her daughter.

"I deserve this. I loved you but was ashamed of you at the same time. I . . . I suppose it's some sort of horrible retribution!"

Sonny put her arms around her mother. "Oh, Mom! No, it's not! I understand how you felt, and I don't hold it against you. Please come live with us. I am going to need help raising these kids with John gone. Won't you please tell me that you will at least consider it?"

Katherine Holloway said nothing but held her daughter as long as she could.

"Now go!" she said. "You have a plane to catch."

Reluctantly, Sonny kissed her mother good-bye and quickly walked out the door. Mrs. Holloway stood on the porch and waved as Sonny's rented car disappeared up the road. Then, in her sorrow, she turned to walk into the house. Theodore, dutifully as always, closed the door behind her and stood stiffly waiting for further orders. Mrs. Holloway began to walk down the long hallway to the morning room when she stopped and turned to Theodore, who was following close behind.

"You know, Theodore . . ." she began.

"Yes, Madame?"

"You do sort of remind me of Boris Karloff!" Mrs. Holloway said with a slight smile and continued down the hallway.

Theodore stood silently for a moment and then shrugged his shoulders.

"Dear me!" he said and followed Mrs. Holloway to the morning room.

Twenty-Two

Mrs. Holloway Has a Surprise

Ever since Brenda's safe return, Mrs. Holloway had become a large part of the Bridges family's lives. The three sisters spent every Saturday at her estate, and she doted over and spoiled Lien at every occasion. Brenda was even able to tease Theodore and force a smile onto his face.

How wrong everyone had been about Mrs. Holloway, and how surprised and humbled they were when she proved to be a good and generous friend! She gave an offering at Thanksgiving to pay for much-needed repairs on the church building and financed a new Sunday school wing. Then one Sunday night, Mrs. Holloway stood up and went forward at the invitation to accept the Lord Jesus as her personal Savior.

As Christmastime drew near, Mrs. Holloway invited the Bridges family over one evening for supper. She told

Mary that she had a surprise for the girls and that they must be sure to come.

Amberley drove everyone to King's Landing in the red Studebaker. As they arrived at the tree-lined drive, everyone was indeed surprised to see a large moving van parked out front. As they made their way into the house, they saw that the rooms and the hallway were cluttered with boxes. Sam and Mary looked at each other but said nothing. Amberley and Brenda saw the boxes and the bare walls and knew that Mrs. Holloway must have decided to leave King's Landing. She had mentioned the possibility once or twice, and now it looked as if it had come to fruition.

After the wonderful supper, Mrs. Holloway asked everyone to repair to the morning room.

"Dear friends," she said once they were all seated around, "I thank you for coming tonight and am very grateful for all the happiness you have brought into my life. I have found the Lord because of you, and for that I am eternally in your debt.

"Today is not only a celebration, but also, I must sadly say, a farewell. I know you are curious about the truck outside and all the boxes strewn throughout the house. I have decided, after some long soul-searching, to sell my estate and move to Indianapolis with my daughter Soon-ei. She's a widow now and needs help rearing her children. I must make sure that they know the Lord, and that necessitates me being there. I am taking Theodore and Thelmy with me also. They have been with me so long that they are a part of my family. I can't and won't leave them behind."

The Bridges family stared at Mrs. Holloway, not knowing what to say.

"Yes, we are leaving King's Landing and Sodus forever. But before I go, I want to give you this."

Mrs. Holloway handed an envelope to Amberley. She turned it over and saw that it was addressed to "Amberley, Brenda, and Lien Bridges."

"Go ahead and open it, dear!" said Mrs. Holloway.

Amberley opened the envelope cautiously and removed the single-page letter. It was printed on the letterhead of a large, well-known law firm in Chicago. Amberley read it aloud.

> Dear Girls,
>
> You have been as dear to me as any daughters could ever be to their mother, and I want to show you my love and gratitude by giving you a gift. I have instructed my attorneys to monitor your progress in school, and all that I ask is that you be good scholars and keep your grades above average. If you will do that, I will promise to pay for your college education at any college or university where you desire to go. A trust fund has been set up in

your names to pay for your tuition and expenses as long as you want to go to school.

With all my love,

K. H. Holloway (Katie)

Brenda and Amberley were speechless. It seemed that the eccentric Mrs. Holloway had now become their great benefactor. Now they would be able to go to college anywhere they liked and concentrate on learning.

Brenda was indeed overwhelmed by Mrs. Holloway's gift. The education she had long coveted and feared she might not get was now brought within her grasp. The pressure to find a job, putting away dimes and quarters so that she could attend just her first semester of college, had instantly vanished. She could now concentrate on getting good grades in high school.

Amberley, on the other hand, felt the pressure of her future as if she had been hit by a bale of hay. No longer could she dillydally and use money as an excuse not to go to college. Amberley had always been a good student, but now, she had been thrown on the rocks. She would have to stop dreaming and grow up overnight.

Lien did not quite understand. Even though she had done well in her studies, school in America had always been a struggle because she had to first learn English. Getting through each day was her care and concern—not an ambiguous college degree that was many years away and might never come.

The girls embraced Mrs. Holloway and thanked her for her far-reaching generosity, each with a different thought of what it meant to her.

Mrs. Holloway embraced them back and tut-tutted as they continued to thank her. "You just see to it that you make me proud of you! I suppose, Brenda, you will become a great educator, and you, Amberley, will become a great Christian author. I am swelled with the anticipation of your success."

Then Mrs. Holloway bid Lien to come and stand by her. She tenderly put her arm around her waist and looked into her deep brown eyes.

"And Lien, my dear, I want you to become a great lady. Never let anyone look down upon you because you are from another land and another culture. My Soon-ei overcame all obstacles and by God's grace, became a doctor. You can do the same."

Mrs. Holloway leaned forward and kissed the young girl on the cheek, gazing upon her face as if she was attempting to memorize every feature. "I shall truly miss you."

* * *

Later that evening when everyone had gone to bed, Amberley sat alone in the living room, reading through a book report she had written for class the next day. It had started to snow around sunset, and several inches had fallen since then. Amberley could hear the wind as it softly rushed past the windows and eves. Finally, reaching up to turn off the light, she closed her notebook and yawned. Sitting in the stillness, she enjoyed the sparkle and glow of the Christmas tree lights against the fluttering snow that blew past the windows. Amberley was getting sleepy, and as she poised to get up, she could hear someone coming down the stairs.

"Doing some last-minute studying?" Dad said as he went to the kitchen and poured what was left of the lukewarm coffee into his cup.

"Yes, sir. Just rereading an assignment for school," Amberley said with a smile.

Sam sat down in his chair and looked at his daughter. "I'm glad you're still up," he said, taking a sip of the strong brew. "It was really something, what Mrs. Holloway did for you girls," he said.

"Oh, yes it was, Daddy. It hasn't yet sunk in."

Sam paused for several moments. "Sweetie, I have been wanting to talk to you about something for awhile, and I guess now is a good time. Firstly, I want you to know that I love you very much, and what I'm going to say is because I love you."

Sam cleared his throat. "All of your life, I've noticed that you have been hesitant to make decisions, to prepare for what's coming. You kind of assume that everything will just iron itself out. I blame myself for most of that. The kind of father I was would make any daughter want to hide under a rock like a crawdad, hanging on to any piece of security and stability that she could find. But now you've been given this wonderful opportunity, this gift. I just don't want to see you miss it. You can't wait until the day after graduation from high school and then decide what you're going to do. You need to meet life head-on and not just wait for it to come to you."

Amberley looked at her father, and tears began to sparkle in her eyes.

"I know that you want to be a Christian writer, and I know you have gifts. But if you don't have determination and resolve, it will never happen. Mrs. Holloway is making it possible for you to get the best education that money can buy. I just want to make sure you understand that."

Amberley looked at her father and knew that he loved her very deeply. She knew that he was trying to address her weaknesses without destroying the joy of Mrs. Holloway's gift. She could see the emotion in his eyes and understood that this little talk had not been easy for him.

Amberley stood up and tucked her notebook under her arm.

"Thank you, Daddy," she said, kissing him on the cheek. "I will not let you down."

Sam smiled. "Now get to bed. Morning and school come early."

"Yes, sir," she said with a grin and quickly walked up the stairs to her bedroom, leaving her father alone in the glow of the Christmas lights.

* * *

The following morning, Amberley said nothing to Brenda about Dad's little talk. It had been something sweet and dear between them, and she would keep it locked up in her heart.

The roads had been freshly plowed, and Brenda chatted about Mrs. Holloway's scholarship as they drove along to school.

"Just think, sis," she said. "I can go to school anywhere I like and study anything I like! Oh, Amber, I can't wait to tell Mrs. Davison. Won't she be surprised?"

Amberley squinted her eyes. "I wonder if we shouldn't be careful who we tell about this. It's like bragging to everybody that we just won a million dollars. Very few people are able to rejoice with others when good things happen to them. They usually just get jealous and hate your guts."

"You're probably right," Brenda said, chuckling at Amberley's bluntness. "Let's keep it under our hats. But I would like to tell Joe."

"It's your call, sis, but I would be careful. Joe already considers you to be almost out of his reach. The thought of you moving away and going to Harvard might really upset him."

"I have no intention of going to Harvard, and Joe knows how I feel. He'll be happy for me."

"Just the same," Amberley said. "I would ease into it if I were you."

At lunch hour that day, Brenda told Joe about Mrs. Holloway's scholarship.

"I'm glad for ya, Brenda," Joe said soberly and sincerely. "I know that it's always been yer dream to go to school."

"I know it's a year and a half away, but I am so excited. It's a dream come true!" Brenda exclaimed.

Joe sat down at a table across from Brenda in the small lunchroom. "I hope everythin' you want happens for ya. Yer the smartest girl I know, and you will help a lotta people."

As they ate their lunches together, Joe was unusually quiet. He finished his sandwich of heavy white bread and homemade farmer's cheese and took a sip of fresh cow's milk from a pint fruit jar.

"Joe, did I upset you?" Brenda asked, noting his silence. "Are you sure it doesn't bother you that I will be going to college?"

Joe packed up his papers and the milk jar and put them into his father's old lunch box. He paused and then looked into Brenda's eyes. "I had been waitin' for the right time to tell you that I wanted you to be my girl, but that time never seemed to come. And after seeing you so excited about college an' all and now this scholarship, I know it wouldn't be right to try and hold ya back."

Brenda was so used to Joe keeping his private thoughts to himself that she was taken off guard by his directness. For a moment, she could only gape.

Joe paused again. "Brenda, I've been studyin' about this thing for some time. You've been through a heap of trouble these last few years, and you deserve ta be happy. It wouldn't be fittin' to keep ya here, scratchin' out a life with a poor old farmer from Shanghai. It would be like keepin' a wild bird in a wire cage when it should be flyin' free. So . . . if I hafta, I am willin' to let you go."

Brenda kept gaping, more shocked than ever. She was so used to Joe fawning over her and going along with everything she wanted like a puppy that she had never expected him to say anything like this.

"But Joe . . . !" she began.

Just then, the school bell rang, announcing the end of lunch hour. Slowly, Brenda and Joe stood up to return to their classes. Neither of them smiled or spoke as they separated in the narrow hallway.

As Brenda sat down and opened her book to begin her next class, her stomach felt numb. Her whole life had been so wrapped around the prospects of going to college and her future that she hadn't considered what her life would be like without Joe.

Twenty-Three
Pleasant It Was

It was springtime again in Sodus Township, and the rapidly melting snow had changed trickling Love Creek into a raging torrent, causing it to run swiftly through Hipps Hollow before rushing into the St. Joseph River. As the breezes began to blow warmly over the hollow and the grass and trees flushed green, Grandma Andrews invited Sam and Mary and the girls over to spend spring break on the farm. The magic of Grandma's farm had been almost ruined by the near tragedy in Buckles Hollow, and a cloud had hung over it ever since. Grandma wanted to remind everyone that it was still a wonderful place to be.

It was a beautiful April morning. Brenda had asked Joe to come over later for supper, but he'd begged off to get an early start on his plowing. Amberley and Lien worked with Ma and Grandma Andrews in the garden, planting potatoes because they would not be harmed by a late frost. Sam spent the morning working with Jeb.

After lunchtime was over and the chores caught up, Amberley sat alone on the porch swing. The air was so warm and pleasant and the sky and clouds so pleasing to the eye that Amberley had to fight back the tears welling in her eyes. She loved the big farm so and dreaded the day when she had to return to school.

Lien brought out a teapot and two cups on a wooden tray and set it on the table in front of the swing. Then she hopped up and snuggled in beside her sister. Amberley took a sip of tea and read aloud to Lien from her book of poems by Longfellow.

> Pleasant it was, when woods were green,
> And winds were soft and low,
> To lie amid some sylvan scene.
> Where, the long drooping boughs between,
> Shadows dark and sunlight sheen
> Alternate come and go;
>
> Or where the denser grove receives
> No sunlight from above,
> But the dark foliage interweaves
> In one unbroken roof of leaves,
> Underneath whose sloping eaves
> The shadows hardly move.

Lien smiled. "This poem reminds me of the hollow, and you promised to take me there sometime soon. Oh, Amber! Can we go there today?"

Amberley pressed her lips together and looked at her sister. "Sweetie, I know you want to go there, to see that place, but it upsets Ma something awful. Can you wait a while longer until she thinks you are ready? Please do it for Ma."

Lien hung her head and nodded. "I will. I do not want to make Ma cry or make her sad. There will be plenty of time. I have my memories now to keep me." But it was clear she was disappointed.

As late afternoon approached, Sam and Jeb came up from the cattle barn to wash up. Grandma rang the dinner bell, announcing that supper was on the table, and the girls hurried inside, famished.

The kitchen was bright and yellow and the table filled with the steaming hot bounty of the farm. A large platter of golden-brown pork steaks graced the very center next to a huge bowl of mashed potatoes dripping from a lagoon of melting butter. There was a dish of buttery lima beans from last summer's garden and a pan of golden acorn squash halves baked with strips of thick bacon and brown sugar.

Amberley noticed a large woven basket on the counter covered with a towel. She threw back the corner, and there were several dozen of Grandma's hot yeast rolls, fresh from the oven. They made her mouth water, and she knew they would be especially good because Grandma had used the same recipe for making her golden-brown loaves of white bread.

Supper was over all too soon, and with the dishes cleared away, the family sat and chatted over coffee, waiting for digestion to make room for dessert later on. Amberley asked to be excused and went outside to sit on the back porch swing. She loved the farm at this time of year, and the hanging swing was her special place. As Amberley enjoyed the falling evening, she heard the screen door open. Brenda came out with a cup of coffee and sat beside her.

"Joe couldn't come?" Amberley asked.

"He has a lot of work to do, getting ready for planting," Brenda said, her tone just a little too defensive. "He is very determined to make his farm work, you know."

Amberley paused. "Is everything all right, sis?"

"Sure, why not?" Brenda quickly answered.

"It's just that you and Joe don't seem to be spending much time together anymore."

"He's just very busy, that's all," Brenda said thoughtfully, dragging her feet as the swing moved back and forth.

The two sisters sat in silence, looking out over the fields. Amberley knew something had happened, but unless Brenda wanted to discuss it, she wouldn't pry.

Life in Old Sodus

The back door opened again, and Sam and Jeb came out with their coffee, discussing yet another maintenance problem in the barn. Mary came out with Grandma Andrews, carrying the pie and plugging in the coffee pot at the outlet on the wall.

"How about letting us in on some of that evening air?" Sam said to Amberley and Brenda with a smile, seating himself next to Jeb. Grandma and Mary dished everyone's dessert up, and at the last, handed Lien a generous piece of apple pie and a scoop of vanilla ice cream. Lien's smile quickly turned to horror when the plate slipped from her fingers and smashed onto the porch floor.

"Oh, my!" Lien jumped up and exclaimed, holding her hands in midair where the plate had been. "Grandma, I am so sorry for breaking your plate and making such a mess. I will clean it up right away!"

"Wait, child!" Grandma said, laughing. "Sit back down. We'll clean it up later. I don't want you feeling uncomfortable here, since this will soon be your new home."

Everyone stopped talking and looked at Grandma, trying to understand what her words meant. She smiled at them all.

"Sam, Mary, I was going to wait until summer to tell you this, but I have decided that I want you and the girls to come and live here with me. I can't take care of the place anymore by myself, and well, I'm kind of lonely. It's going to be yours anyway. Why not now?"

Jeb stood up and politely put down his plate and cup. "'Scuse me, Miss Marian. I'll be goin' to my cabin now."

"Jeb, you just sit back down, now! This concerns you too. I have no secrets from you."

Jeb slowly sank back into his seat, just as puzzled as the rest of them.

"Ma, are you all right? Is there something you're not telling us?" Mary asked with a worried look.

"Oh, no, no, I'm as fit as a fiddle," Grandma answered, smiling. "I just want my family around me, that's all. I have been thinking on this for a long time and would have asked you sooner except for Sam's bullheadedness."

"But Ma," Sam said. "My job's in Eau Claire, and now I have a chance to buy the business from my boss."

Mary looked at her husband with her mouth open.

He smiled sheepishly. "Sorry, Mary. Tom Enkins just asked me today, and I didn't have a chance to talk to you about it. He wants to retire after this season. But getting back to the issue at hand," Sam continued, turning back to Grandma Andrews, "what would I do with this huge farm?"

"What do you think, Sam Bridges?" Grandma said. "This farm was once quite an operation, and with the right touch and the right man, it can be again. I know what you've been doing for the Schenkle boy. You've got his farm organized and running like a charm. You can do it here too."

"I don't know, Mom. This is much too sudden. Mary and I will have to talk it over."

"Mary has always wanted to live on the old farm, Sam," Grandma said. "She loves this place but never told you because she knew you wouldn't listen. If you are worried about me trying to boss you around, that is not a problem, because I have already signed over the deed to you and Mary. All I want to do is live out the rest of my life around my family and get to know my grandchildren and someday my great-grandchildren."

"Mary, is it true? Have you always wanted to live on the farm?" Sam asked.

Mary paused and looked into Sam's eyes.

"Sam, I love this old place. I never wanted to leave it ever. My dream was to live here with you and raise our family. I never said anything to you because I didn't want to make our life any more complicated. I was sure you would look at it as charity and say no forever."

Sam thought for a moment and then turned to Grandma Andrews.

"So you think this place has a chance to become a going operation again?"

"At one time, this place supplied part of Berrien County with a good chunk of its dairy products. It can be whatever you want to make it, Sam."

Sam squinted his eyes and tightened his jaw in deep thought. This was one he hadn't figured.

"It would be quite a challenge. It wasn't so long ago that they wouldn't hire me at the fruit exchange sorting apples. Now I am faced with the decision of owning my own construction company or taking over a huge farm operation." He shook his head with a bit of a laugh, but they could all see the pressure on him. "But Mom," he said abruptly, putting his cup down on the table to face her. "I feel kind of strange inheriting something you and Pa worked so hard to build. I have put no sweat equity into it. Is it right?"

"Samuel Bridges, what do you mean?" Grandma scolded. "You have been a good and faithful husband to my daughter and have made her happy. You are raising three wonderful girls who are sweeter than sugar pie. Okay, you had a rocky road for a few years, but that's over. You are as dear to me as any of my children, and most of all, I love you and trust you."

Grandma Andrews paused. "Sam, you are so concerned with earning everything that you don't know how to just accept a gift. Sometimes, a gift is just as beneficial to the giver as the receiver."

Mary and Grandma and the girls wiped their eyes. Jeb blinked, listening intently. He wondered how this would all affect him.

"Now let's talk no more of this tonight. You and Mary pray on it, and I'll abide by your decision. I didn't mean to throw a damper on another picnic," Grandma said, handing Lien another plate of pie and ice cream.

* * *

It was late evening of the last day at Grandma's, and an orange sun lay low in the western sky over Lake Michigan. The family walked together up the path leading to the small graveyard on the hill adjacent to the ancient apple orchard. They could see from a distance the weathered wooden crosses and marble headstones that marked their small family cemetery, signifying the past generations of the Andrews family. Amberley saw a small headstone with the name Sanders. This was where they had buried Jeb's wife and child.

Near the base of a very old apple tree was a smooth red granite stone without any markings. Grandma drew near to Lien and put her arm around her small shoulders.

"This is where we buried your folks, child. Right here with our family. The stone is not marked because we did not know their names. We thought that perhaps you could help us out with that, since you are older now and can tell us what to write."

Lien slowly walked to the place and knelt in the cool grass. She felt along the smooth stone with her hands, as would a blind person attempting to see with her fingers. Lien began to weep softly, venting the grief that had been held somewhere deep within her soul. Everyone stood reverently and patiently until finally, Mary went over and knelt beside her.

Lien finally stood up and then spoke something in Vietnamese. As they made their way down the old orchard hill, Lien walked on ahead and went into the house.

"What did she say, Sam?" Mary whispered.

"She said, 'I thank you, my mother and father, for your love and for giving your lives to save me. You have made me a perfect picture of the love of Jesus. I will never forget you.'"

They all wiped the moisture from their eyes as Grandma spoke.

"I will make arrangements to have the stone carved out proper."

THE END